Koinonia

A Place for Tough and Tender Love

ii

Koinonia

A Place for Tough and Tender Love

JIMMY JIVIDEN

This book has been designed to be used for group study as well as for your personal use.

GOSPEL ADVOCATE CO.
P. O. BOX 150
NASHVILLE, TN 37202

Published by the Gospel Advocate Co.
P.O. Box 150, Nashville, TN

ISBN 0-89225-469-6

Acknowledgements

I acknowledge the debt I owe to so many who have helped to make this book possible. Many of those from whom I have learned are listed in the endnotes. Some of the basic concepts contained in this work were first set forth in two series of lectures and published by Star Bible under the title of *Caring Enough to Correct*. Stimulation to finish my research came about from the practical needs of the church to understand the scope and limits of fellowship in Christ.

The completion of this work would have been impossible were it not for the help of those who from the very first have corrected errors, offered helpful suggestions and sharpened my focus in needed areas. I am particularly indebted to Phil and Boots Nichols, Everett Ferguson, Clark Potts, James Baird, Edward Myers and Dale Huff who have critiqued the entire manuscript. Others have given help in specific areas. Among them are Howard Norton, Cecil May, Ed Wharton and Don Humphrey. Special appreciation is extended to Edward Myers who prepared the questions at the end of each chapter.

My three children, Steve, Diane and Debbie, and their spouses, Marta, Dale and James, have all played a part in the final preparation. My wife, Shirley, has been both a helper and enabler in every stage of writing. It is to her and my family that I dedicate this work.

Jimmy Jividen
February 1989

Foreword

Fellowship is essential to the working of acceptable Christianity. Jesus is portrayed in the gospels in such winsome terms that being in His presence throughout eternity becomes the supreme motive for our lives. Otherwise the promise, "there you may be also,"[1] would be void of meaning as would His statement "and lo, I am with you always, even unto the end of the world."[2]

In the midst of an ecumenical climate in which honorable disagreement over religious differences is considered poor form, a new book entitled *Koinonia* is a little surprising. However, after reading Jimmy Jividen's work you may feel like repeating the catch phrase of the television commerical, "Thanks, I needed that!"

Brother Jividen raises early in the book some of the tough questions we face in the brotherhood regarding fellowship. These include:

1. What should be the correct response of Christians to the current dialogue between members of churches of Christ and the Conservative Christian Churches?

2. What should be the attitude toward those churches under the authority of the Boston Church?

3. What about the tension between so-called "discipling churches" and "mainline churches?"

4. What is the relationship between those churches labeled "non-cooperative" and "institutional"?

Koinonia

Although raising these questions, the author does not fall into the trap of attempting to make the work a ready reference volume that gives a quick answer to every complex issue on the subject. Instead, he uses the light of the Scripture to bring into sharper focus the true meaning of fellowship with its blessings and its limits.

Jimmy is in no sense apologetic about the fact that in the past we have been willing to withdraw fellowship. On the contrary, he would agree in principle with Thomas Campbell's action, shortly before he left Scotland for America, in breaking fellowship with the Seceeder Presbyterian Church because of doctrinal differences. He understands fellowship to be:

...a sphere of spiritual existence based on one's
relationship with all of God's children in the church.
It is more than a mere experiential feeling grounded in
subjective emotionalism that is above reason. It is a
real knowledge grounded in actual obedience that can
be tested by objective standards.

In effect, we must not become so flaccid about doctrinal convictions that nothing seems important enough to cause a break in fellowship.

When we read of the members of the first church selling their goods and possessions in order that none would be hungry, we have to confess there are depths of Christian fellowship which we have not yet begun to plumb. We can stifle our collective conscience in this, but, as Andrew Jackson's schoolboy classmate reminisced of wrestling the backwood's stripling, "I could throw him every time but he wouldn't stay throwed," similarly our consciences will not stay stifled regarding fellowship.

Jimmy Jividen is much more skillful in the use of words than most of us. This is one of those books you will want to read with a highlighter in your hand because there are so many memorable statements. For instance, "A Christian does not decide whom he wants to include in fellowship and whom he wants to exclude from fellowship. He only recognizes what God has already determined." And, in speaking of the fellowship of the church, he quotes Hans Kung's insightful statement, "Man is removed from the loneliness of his own ego, and finds a home in community."

The writer brings to this book a seasoned Christian view. By his own experience he is comfortable with the sublime qualities of the Christian way and brings a deep Christian perspective to the fore as he explores fellowship in a thoroughly biblical manner. Jimmy Jividen writes with cool dispassionate logic and the book focuses in an orderly way on almost every conceivable dimension of the subject.

In my judgment, this book will have a long and useful life. The closing two chapters, "The Process of Discipline" and "The Purposes of Discipline," are alone worth the price of the book. Elders and church leaders will find themselves reading and then rereading this book for the biblical insight it gives into this vital subject.

Thanks, Jimmy, we needed this.

James O. Baird
Chancellor
Oklahoma Christian College

[1]John 14:6.
[2]Matthew 28:20.

Koinonia

x

Table of Contents

Koinonia

Introduction

"It would be tragic to have been wrong about 'Fellowship in Christ' at the Judgment."

The New Testament teaching on "fellowship in Christ" has deep spiritual meaning, involves far-reaching theological implications and demands radical practical action. Like *agape* love which motivates it, "fellowship in Christ" is entwined in, around and through both one's relationship to Christ and His church.

One cannot be in "fellowship with Christ" and out of fellowship with His church. One cannot be in the favor of God the Father and out of favor with His children. One cannot have communion with the Holy Spirit without having communion with all of those in whom He dwells.

"Fellowship in Christ" is serious business. It is not to be extended without caution. It is not to be denied without cause.

There are factors involved in extending or denying "fellowship in Christ" which cannot be known in the absolute sense. The motives of a person's heart and the integrity of his faith cannot be measured by the frailties of one's own personal judgment.

1

There are factors involved in extending or denying "fellowship in Christ" which can be known. One can know the truth revealed in the Scriptures. One can observe and know the actions of a man's life. The fruit of a man's life can be compared to the truth of the Scriptures. Such will determine his relationship to God. His relationship with God will then determine his relationship in the church.

"Fellowship in Christ" cannot be extended or denied on the basis of subjective personal judgment. It must be extended or denied upon the basis of conduct that can be objectively discerned in his life.

It would be tragic to have been wrong about "fellowship in Christ" at the Judgment. One must not be so exclusive as to deny fellowship on earth to those whom the Lord accepts at the Judgment. One must not be so inclusive as to extend fellowship on earth to those whom the Lord will not accept at the Judgment.

Some who claim to follow Christ will be guilty of denying fellowship to others on the basis of social and economic criteria. They will not only be embarrassed for their error but will also be condemned to everlasting destruction because of it. Jesus said:

> Truly I say to you, to the extent that you did not do it to
> one of the least of these, you did not do it to me. And
> these will go away into eternal punishment.[1]

Some who claim to follow Christ will be guilty of denying fellowship to others on the basis of party politics. They either refuse "to receive the brethren" like Diotrephes who loved "to be first among them," or else they are afraid to go against the threats of a church boss who threatens to "put them out of the church."[2]

Some who claim to follow Christ will be guilty of extending fellowship to those who have broken fellowship with God. This seemed to be the case of some of the Christians in the church at Corinth. In perverted puffed up pride they were extending fellowship to a brother living in an adulterous union. They no doubt prided themselves in being liberated from the sexual hangups of a legalistic past. Paul used strong language and demanded drastic action to correct the situation.

> And you have become arrogant, and have not mourned
> instead, in order that the one who had done this deed
> might be removed from your midst... deliver such a

2

one to Satan... clean out the old leaven... not to
associate with immoral people... not even to eat
with such a one... remove the wicked man from among
yourselves.[3]

Some who claim to follow Christ will be guilty of extending fellowship to those who are not even Christians in the New Testament sense. Their fellowship is open to anyone who appears to be sincere and satisfied in his own mind that he is a Christian. There is no testing of their understanding or the spirit that they follow. They are accepted because they call Jesus "Lord, Lord" rather than because they have done the will of the Father in Heaven.[4]

The loosening of the limits of fellowship might, in a temporary way, make for greater numbers or avoid some difficult confrontations, but such does not change the standard for fellowship in the New Testament.

The Restoration Movement has always seemed to have some who emphasized unity to the exclusion of doctrine. To them, ecclesiastical union accomplished by democratic compromise is greater than Divine unity achieved by full allegiance to Christ. Anyone who has been immersed for any reason can join their fellowship. There is even a category for being a "brother in prospect" if one has not been baptized.

There was error and misunderstanding about fellowship in the first century churches. The same is true today. The inspired teachings given in the New Testament to resolve fellowship problems are just as relevant today.

Some very important questions facing Christians today revolve around the nature and extent of "fellowship in Christ."

What is the scope and limit of "fellowship in Christ"?
What objective criteria determines fellowship?

Is there a difference between fellowship in the church
and sonship to God? Can one be a child of God and out of
fellowship with the church?

Is there a Scriptural basis and method for exercising
discipline in the church?

Why are there barriers between brothers because of social,
educational, sectional, economic and ethnic diversities?
Why are there barriers between congregations? Can one
congregation withdraw from another congregation?

What should be the correct response of Christians to the
current dialogue between members of churches of Christ
and the Conservative Christian Churches? What should be
the attitude toward those churches under the authority
of the Boston Church? What about the tension between
what are sometimes labeled "discipling churches" and
"mainline churches"? What is the relationship between
those churches labeled "non-cooperative" and "institutional"?

This book is written in response to such needs and questions. The author
does not presume to know all of the answers but hopes that this material will
cause the discussion of these issues to become more Scriptural than social,
more doctrinal than dramatic, more contemporary than historical and more
actual than theoretical.

Endnotes

[1]Matthew 25:45-46.
[2]III John 9-10.
[3]I Corinthians 5:2, 5, 7, 9, 11, 13.
[4]Matthew 7:21-22.

Section 1
The Nature of Fellowship

The nature of fellowship in Christ can be best understood by first viewing it from different perspectives. When this is done, one must then bring the different perspectives together into a total picture. This is the purpose of Section I.

Chapter one is a linguistic study of fellowship. The different shades of meaning found in the *koinon* group of words are examined in the *koine* period of the Greek language. Such a study reveals its deep meaning.

Chapter two is a theological study of fellowship. The theological basis for fellowship in the church is shown to be grounded in a spiritual relationship with God. Such a study shows its holiness.

Chapter three is an examination of the analogies used in the New Testament to describe fellowship in Christ. This study focuses on the needs and responsibilites of fellowship in the church.

Chapter four is a study of the different expressions of fellowship reflected in the life of the early church. Such a study demonstrates the need to restore both the meaning and practice of genuine fellowship in Christ in the twentieth century church.

1/Definitions

"If God is one's father, then all of
God's children are his brothers."
"Brotherhood involves all those who
are children of God by rights of birth."

The discussion of any topic must begin with the definition of terms. If terms are not understood in the same way by those involved in the discusssion, it will only result in misunderstanding and confusion. Disagreements between two parties are often resolved when each understands what the other means by the use of some term. The same English term "football" has an entirely different meaning to an American than it does to one who lives in England.

It is particularly important to define the New Testament concept of "fellowship" because of its colloquial use. Two current uses of this term cloud the New Testament meaning.

Fellowship often means little more than a social activity. One often hears references to "after-church fellowship," "fellowship room," "fellowship committee" and "fellowship meal" in a context in which it means only social activity.[1] Such a use of the term is a prelude to the smell of coffee brewing.

Koinonia

Fellowship often is used as a term to describe ecclesiastical sanctions or barriers.[2] A congregation is "out of fellowship." This means that some other congregations do not sanction their activities or teachings. Sometimes one is asked, "Do you fellowship a certain group?" Such a question is difficult to answer if it is not known how the "fellowship" is understood by the questioner.

Even though these uses of the term are related to the New Testament concept, they do not present the total picture.

Koinonia

The understanding of the Greek term, *koinonia*, is necessary to understand the New Testament idea of fellowship. It is translated "fellowship," "communion" and even "contribution." The *koinon* group of words of which it is a part has a varied use in the New Testament.[3]

It sometimes refers to sharing with someone in something. Jesus shared in the flesh and blood of humanity.[4]

It sometimes refers to participation in or identification with Christ. The Corinthian Christians were called into fellowship with Christ.[5] They identified with Jesus in a spiritual communion.

It sometimes refers to the partaking of the Lord's Supper in which Christians share in the blood and body of Christ.[6]

It refers to the spiritual partnership between Paul and Philemon. Paul extends this partnership to Onesimus by asking Philemon to receive his runaway slave as a brother.[7]

It refers to the collection taken by the church to assist other brethren.[8] It involves the spirit of generous sharing as contrasted with the spirit of selfish getting. It is even translated "contribution" in one instance.[9]

It refers to the formal extension of fellowship to those of the common faith. Paul and Barnabas received the "right hand of fellowship."[10]

The *koin*-group of words is used in varied contexts in the New Testament and has many shades of meaning. All of these meanings involve sharing, participation, fellowship or communion. Such reflect the essence of the word group. Glenn Kramar gave the following conclusion from his study of the *koinonia*:

The *koin*- family of words, which in classical and
Koine Greek was essentially secular in usage, with

occasional religious usages, was adopted by the New
Testament writers to express rich spiritual
relationships characteristic of Christianity. This
family was appropiate for this because of "its capacity
for conveying the sense of an inward union."[11]

General Meaning

The term, *koinonia* , is broader than its religious meaning. It is used with
reference to all kinds of fellowships.

It can refer to a business fellowship. Peter, James and John were part-
ners[12] in the fishing business.[13]

It can refer to a domestic fellowship. The sharing between husband and
wife is *koinonia* in literature of the first century. This is not the same *koinonia* that
is found in Christian fellowship. There can be a domestic fellowship without
an "in Christ" fellowship. The Christian wife is instructed to maintain her role
in her domestic fellowship even though her unbelieving husband does not
know a fellowship in Christ.[14]

It can refer to a social fellowship. In the context of forbidding an "in
Christ" fellowship with an immoral brother, Paul taught Christians that they
could maintain their social contact with immoral people of the world.

I wrote you in my letter not to associate with immoral
people; I did not at all mean with the immoral people of
this world, or with the covetous and swindlers, or with
idolaters; for then you would have to go out of the world.
But actually, I wrote to you not to associate with any so-
called brother if he should be an immoral person... [15]

The social contact with immoral people of the world was something one could
not avoid while living in the world. Christians do not have an "in Christ"
fellowship with unbelievers. The participation Christians have with them is
social, business, domestic, etc. There is no spiritual tie. The case is different
with those who are Christians. The spiritual fellowship which binds Christians
together is stronger, warmer and deeper than secular bonds. It requires more
to maintain it. There is a sense in which "all things are common." It even
demands severe action if the fellowship is threatened. The nature of an "in
Christ" fellowship is such that when it is broken, it demands a social exclusion
of the offending brother.

People in New Testament times were involved in various kinds of fellowship. The bonds which held these fellowships together were different and involved varied degrees of committment.

Sometimes these non-religious fellowships proved helpful to the early Christians. Paul used his political ties as a Roman citizen to his advantage.

Sometimes fellowship ties with non-Christians proved destructive. Paul warned the Corinthians about this.

> Do not be bound together with unbelievers; for what
> partnership have righteousness and lawlessness, or
> what fellowship has light with darkness?[16]

The New Testament practice would suggest that non-Christian associations were not wrong *per se* , but the basis, the demands and the priorities of these associations could make them wrong.

One could have a political association in addition to his "in Christ" fellowship. Erastus' political connections as a city treasurer did not compromise his "in Christ" fellowship.[17]

One could have a domestic partnership without an "in Christ" fellowship. A Christian was admonished not to break a domestic relationship with a spouse just because he was an unbeliever.[18]

An "in Christ" fellowship does not nullify other fellowships unless such a relationship demands compromise.[19]

New Testament Description

One can understand the New Testament teachings on fellowship by observing the way it was practiced in the early church. A number of "snapshots" of the fellowship experienced by the first Christians are found in Acts. They reflect the nature, warmth and depth of their fellowship.

> And all those who had believed were together, and had all
> things in common; and they began selling their property
> and possessions, and were sharing them with all, as anyone
> might have need. And day by day continuing with one mind
> in the temple, and breaking bread from house to house, they
> were taking their meals together with gladness and sincerity
> of heart...[20]

Notice the words in bold type. They reflect the meaning of fellowship in the Jerusalem church.

This fellowship was not hampered by persecution. Luke described the fellowship of the church after the apostles were jailed for preaching.

> And the congregation of those who believed were of one
> heart and soul; and not one of them claimed that anything
> belonging to him was his own; but all things were common
> property to them.[21]

A spirit of oneness was so reflected in their fellowship that self was forgotten for the benefit of others.

Notice three things in this verse that help one to understand the nature of an "in Christ" fellowship. First, those involved in the fellowship were believers. Second, those in fellowship were united. They had only one heart and one soul because they were one body. Third, they were unselfish. Self ownership ceased, and their possessions were regarded as common property. It was one for all and all for one.

The New Testament shows that sometimes the bonds of fellowship in the early church weakened with time. Those who once unselfishly committed themselves and their fortunes to the fellowship had to be reminded that their fellowship had grown cold. The writer of Hebrews expressed this admonition.

> But remember the former days, when, after being
> enlightened, you endured a great conflict of sufferings,
> partly, by being made a public spectacle through
> reproaches and tribulations, and partly by becoming sharers
> with those who were so treated. For you showed sympathy
> to the prisoners, and accepted joyfully the seizure of your
> property, knowing that you have for yourselves a better
> possession and an abiding one.[22]

Fellowship involved identifying with brethren in persecution. It involved enduring the reproaches of being a follower of Christ. It involved joyfully giving up possessions because you were connected with Christ and His church.

It is hard to understand how a fellowship which had cost so much in the past could have been lightly esteemed by the recipients of Hebrews. Perhaps the answer is to be found in the fact they had been neglecting fellowship. They had to be reminded to...

...encourage one another day after day, as long as it is
still called "Today," lest any one of you be hardened by
the deceitfulness of sin.[23]

and let us consider how to stimulate one another to love and
good deeds, not forsaking our own assembling together,
as is the habit of some, but encouraging one another...[24]

The neglect of practicing fellowship and encouraging one another in fellowship had allowed their faith to grow cold.

"In Christ" Fellowship

Fellowship in the New Testament is better understood when it is understood as an "in Christ" relationship.[25] One is baptized into Christ and by this
means obtains a new relationship to God. He becomes a son.[26] This new
relationship breaks down barriers which exist between men and brings all into
a oneness "in Christ."[27] This new life "in Christ" begins at baptism at which time
one joins with Christ in His death, burial and resurrection. Paul described it
thus:

Or do you not know that all of us who have been baptized
into Christ Jesus have been baptized into His death?
Therefore we have been buried with Him through baptism
into death, in order that as Christ was raised from the dead
through the glory of the Father, so we too might walk in
newness of life.[28]

There is new life in Christ which involves a new relationship with God. This
new relationship makes one "dead to sin, but alive to God in Christ Jesus."[29]
One dwells in a new sphere of existence after he has experienced this new life
in Christ.

Paul further describes this new sphere of existence as being a place where
there is reconciliation and fellowship between God and man in Jesus Christ.

Therefore if any man is in Christ, he is a new creature; the
old things passed away; behold, new things have come. Now

12

all these things are from God, who reconciled us to Himself
through Christ...[30]

This new life in Christ involves fellowship with God and all of His children.
Being "in Christ" removes estrangement from all parties. It is because of the
nature of this "in Christ" fellowship that it must not be lightly esteemed or
carelessly broken.

Closely connected to the concept of an "in Christ" fellowship in Paul's
writings is the connection of *"en "* with "fellowship" in the writings of John.[31]
Again there is emphasis on the Divine nature of this fellowship. Again there
is emphasis upon the blood of Christ being the means by which sin is removed,
and fellowship with God and one another is possible.

If we say that we have fellowship with Him and yet walk
in darkness, we lie and do not practice the truth; but if we
walk in the light as He Himself is in the light, we have
fellowship with one another, and the blood of Jesus His Son
cleanses us from all sin.[32]

An "in Christ" connection to fellowship shows the theological basis by which
one can be reconciled to God. Christ erased the estrangement caused by sin and
allowed sinful men again to know Divine fellowship. This "in Christ" fellowship is the realm of existence where one lives when he becomes a "new
creature" at baptism. This fellowship not only erases estrangement between
God and man but also between all other men in this realm of fellowship. They
become brothers because they are sons of God.

Brotherhood and Fellowship

Brotherhood and fellowship are not the same. One can have a brother
who is not in fellowship. If that brother has broken fellowship with God by sin
and error, then the rest of God's children are not to extend fellowship to him.
He is still a child of God. One cannot be "un-brothered." He might be an erring,
alienated brother who is out of fellowship, but he is still a brother.

One becomes a son of God when he is born into the family of God at
baptism.[33] Because of this sonship, he immediately and automatically becomes
a brother to every other child of God. If God is one's father, then all of God's
children are his brothers.

Christians do not choose who their brothers will be. They only recognize as brothers those who have been born into the family of God. Brotherhood has nothing to do with ethnic background, social strata, economic level, educational attainment or personal interests. It has everything to do with one's relationship with God.

Christians in every age have had problems with this. The first century Christian had problems in accepting as brothers those of different races and different social status. Jews would not eat with Gentiles even though they were brethren.[34] There were sometimes barriers between the rich and poor[35] and the masters and slaves.[36] These barriers were wrong and had to be torn down. Brotherhood rests solely and wholly on whether or not one has been born into the family of God.

> There is neither Jew nor Greek, there is neither slave
> nor free man, there is neither male nor female; for you are
> all one in Christ Jesus.[37]

Brotherhood includes all of God's children by rights of birth. There can not be different levels of brotherhood or different brotherhoods in God's family.

Fellowship is different from brotherhood. It is true that one can not know an "in Christ" fellowship with one unless he is a brother. It is not true that all brothers have an "in Christ" fellowship.

Within the brotherhood of God's family are different kinds of children. Even though they are children, not all know the fellowship of God nor are they to be included in the fellowship of God's family, the church.

There are prodigal sons who have left the fellowship of the Father's house to live in moral rebellion. They are not in fellowship with the Father or God's family because of their own choice. They are brothers because they are children of God. They are not in fellowship because they have chosen to leave the family.

There are erring brethren[38] and sinful brethren[39] who need to be restored to the fellowship. Their false faith and sinful lives have alienated them from God. They are still God's children, but they are not in fellowship with God or His children.

There are brethren who have left the fellowship. They were at one time a part of the fellowship but came to believe they had outgrown it. Such was the case of those refuted by John.

They went out from us, but they were not really of us; for
if they had been of us, they would have remained with us;
but they went out, in order that it might be shown that
they all are not of us.[40]

It is unclear whether these were false brethren who were never really a part of God's family or whether they were at one time in God's family but felt that they were above the fellowship of God's other children who were not as spiritual as they were. One thing is clear. They had left the fellowship even though they claimed to know God.[41]

There are brethren who have been disciplined by the church. Such was the case in Corinth.[42] A brother in the church had his father's wife. Paul corrects the Corinthians because they were tolerating this brother to remain in their fellowship. He does not deny that this immoral brother is a child of God, but he demands that such a one be put out of the fellowship of the church.

Fellowship is narrower than brotherhood. Brotherhood involves all those who are children of God by rights of birth. Fellowship in Christ does not include anyone outside the brotherhood, but neither does it include all who are in the brotherhood. Immoral brethren, erring brethren, sinful brethren and those who have chosen to leave the fellowship are excluded. They are not excluded by the authority of the church. They are excluded from Divine fellowship by the authority of God. The church only recognizes what God has done.

Endnotes

[1] The New Testament idea of fellowship does often involve the sharing of a meal and the social aspects surrounding it. See Acts 2:46. Limiting fellowship to mere social activity however robs it of its full meaning.

[2] This use of fellowship is also biblical. Luke used it when referring to Paul and Barnabas receiving the "right hand of fellowship" from James, Cephas and John. See Galatians 2:9. The New Testament use of the term is much broader than this use.

[3] Friedrick Hauck, "*Koinonia* ", TDNT Vol. III, pp. 797-809.

[4] Hebrews 2:14.

[5] I Corinthians 1:9.

[6] I Corinthians 10:16.

[7] Philemon 17.

[8]Philippians 4:15.
[9]II Corinthians 9:13.
[10]Galatians 2:9.
[11]Glenn Gordon Kramar, *Koinonia and Its Cognates as Related to Fellowship in the New Testament* (unpublished Master's thesis, Abilene Christian College, 1966), p. 25.
[12]*koinonoi* is the term used.
[13]Luke 5:10.
[14]I Peter 3:1. See also I Corinthians 7:12-16.
[15]I Corinthians 5:9-11.
[16]II Corinthians 6:14.
[17]Romans 16:23.
[18]I Corinthians 7:13-15.
[19]II Corinthians 6:14-16.
[20]Acts 2:44-46.
[21]Acts 4:32.
[22]Hebrews 10:32-34.
[23]Hebrews 3:13.
[24]Hebrews 10:24-25.
[25]The concept of being "in Christ" is not found prior to Paul and is nearly unique with his writings. See Albrecht Oepke, *"en "*, TDNT, Vol. II, pp. 541-542.
[26]Galatians 3:27.
[27]Galatians 3:28.
[28]Romans 6:3-4.
[29]Romans 6:11.
[30]II Corinthians 5:17-18.
[31]Albrecht Oepke, *op . cit .*, p. 543 notes that John is unique in connecting *"en "* and "fellowship."
[32]I John 1:6-7.
[33]John 3:3-5. See also Galatians 3:26-28.
[34]Galatians 2:12-14.
[35]I Corinthians 11:22.
[36]I Timothy 6:1-2.
[37]Galatians 3:28. See also I Corinthians 12:13 and Colossians 3:11.
[38]James 5:19.
[39]Galatians 6:1.
[40]I John 2:19.
[41]I John 2:3-6 shows that they claimed to know God without keeping the

word or Jesus' commandments. John declared them liars because such an understanding of knowing God was not true.
[42]I Corinthians 5:1-13.

Study Questions:

1. Discuss the word "koinonia."

2. What is the New Testament description of fellowship?

3. What is the significance of the phrase "in Christ" in relationship to the word fellowship?

4. Is there a difference between brotherhood and fellowship? What, if any, is that difference and how is it distinguished?

5. What is implied in terms of relationship to those "in Christ"?

6. Is fellowship more narrow than brotherhood? Why or why not?

Koinonia

2/ Theological Basis of Fellowship

"The cross that bridged the gap of alienation between God and man also bridged the gap of alienation between man and man."

"When a brother looks at me with all my weaknesses and warts, he does not turn his back because he is looking through Jesus."

Fellowship in Christ is the strongest tie that can exist among men. It is greater than any earthly tie. The reason for this is that it is based upon a Divine relationship. It is in a spiritual realm of existence and is not bound in time.

Quest for this fellowship can cause a man to turn his back on sins which have enslaved his life. It can cause him to walk away from longtime relationships which would draw him away from this spiritual tie. Work relationships, social connections, family ties and the bonds of friendship all pale in comparison to this "in Christ" fellowship.

Loyalty to this fellowship supercedes all other relationships in life, because it is connected to Christ. It was this loyalty which caused Simon and Andrew to walk away from their fishing boats and follow Jesus.[1] It was this loyalty that caused Matthew to leave his tax collecting booth.[2] It was this loyalty that caused Paul to say "forgetting what lies behind"[3] and "I count all things to be loss in view of the surpassing value of knowing Christ Jesus my Lord."[4]

19

In discussing the priority that His followers must place on their relationship with Him, Jesus said:

> If anyone comes to Me, and does not hate his own father and mother and wife and children and brothers and sisters, yes, and even his own life, he cannot be My disciple.
>
> Whoever does not carry his own cross and come after Me cannot be My disciple.
>
> So therefore, no one of you can be My disciple who does not give up all his own possessions.[5]

The ties of fellowship in the church are as strong and as demanding as one's relationship to Jesus Himself.

The ties of this fellowship are more enduring than any fleshly ties. They go beyond time into eternity. Friendship ties cannot endure beyond the grave except in fading memories. Domestic ties will not exist in heaven.[6] Those fleshly ties involving relationships at work and play change and pass away with time. Ties to institutions, clubs, governments and societies loosen as both we and they change because of different needs. The ties of Christian fellowship do not so soon pass. They endure because they are not bound in time and space. After this world disintegrates into the nothingness from whence it was created, Christians will still be "sons of God" and "brothers" to all of God's children. The ties of Christian fellowship are timeless and eternal.

The very nature of the "in Christ" fellowship makes it deeper and more real than any other relationship. It is a spiritual tie. It involves more than the physical features of one's body. It is deeper than the social graces of one's personality. It is broader than the scope of interest and intellectual aptitude that one has. It involves the spirit—that part of a man which is his real identity. It is from the spirit of man that come the decisions of his will. It is this unique spirit of a man which is joined into fellowship with God and all of His children.

Grounded in Divinity

Fellowship "in Christ" is grounded in Divinity. Though it may be desired by man, yet it can only be accomplished by God. God is the initiator and the sustainer of this fellowship.

Fellowship is based on being in God's family. The only way one can call God, "Abba Father," is to be His son. Sonship is possible only by God's initiative.

First, one is begotten by the Father through the word. Such is the language of the Scriptures.

> In the exercise of His will He brought us forth by the word
> of truth, so that we might be as it were the first fruits
> among His creatures.[7]

> for you have been born again not of seed which is perishable
> but imperishable, that is, through the living and abiding
> word of God.[8]

Second, one is born again of the water and the Spirit. Such is the language of the Scriptures.

> Jesus answered and said to him, "Truly, truly, I say to you,
> unless one is born again, he cannot see the kingdom of God."
> ....unless one is born of the water and the Spirit, he cannot
> enter into the kingdom of God.[9]

To become one of God's children, one must be begotten by God through the word and born of the water and the Spirit. This new birth puts him into the family of God. Only then can he know fellowship as a son of God.

Fellowship is based upon being reconciled to God. This reconcilation cannot be accomplished on man's own initiative. He has sinned and cannot come into God's fellowship in such an unholy state. The holiness of God and the defilement of sin are mutually exclusive. What can man do? Nothing! He finds himself without God and without hope.

It was into this dilemma that Jesus came. He became man. He experienced flesh and blood. He was tempted and tried and endured pain and death. He fully identified with the predicament of man[10] but remained sinless.[11] He went to the Cross on behalf of man and accomplished reconciliation with God. Those who are "in Christ" are reconciled to God.

> Therefore if any man is in Christ, he is a new creature;
> the old things passed away; behold, new things have come.
> Now all these things are from God, who reconciled us to

Himself through Christ, and gave us the ministry of
reconciliation, namely, that God was in Christ reconciling
the world to Himself, not counting their trespasses
against them...[12]

He made Him who knew no sin to be sin on our behalf, that
we might become the righteousness of God in Him.[13]

Fellowship with God is based on man's reconciliation to God in Christ. Man's
fellowship with God is based on Divine initiative, not human merit.

The reconciliation with God, made possible in Christ, has further implications. It involves the theological basis of the fellowship that should exist
between men. The cross that bridged the gap of alienation between God and
man also bridged the gap of alienation between man and man. Not only did
Christ make fellowship possible with God, but He also made possible fellowship between men. This was the message Paul gave to show the theological
basis of fellowship between Jews and Gentiles.

But now in Christ Jesus you who formerly were far off
have been brought near by the blood of Christ. For He
Himself is our peace, who made both groups into one, and
broke down the barrier of the dividing wall, by abolishing
in His flesh the enmity, which is the Law of commandments
contained in ordinances, that in Himself He might make the
two into one new man, thus establishing peace, and might
reconcile them both in one body to God through the cross,
by it having put to death the enmity.[14]

Fellowship with God and others is only possible through the cross of Christ.
When God looks at defiled, sinful man, He is not repulsed because He is
looking though Jesus. When a brother looks at me with all my weaknesses and
warts, he does not turn his back because he is looking through Jesus. The only
theological possibility of fellowship between men is "in Christ."

Fellowship is based on the indwelling of the Holy Spirit. In the context of
emphasizing the fellowship of the church under the analogy of the human
body, Paul affirms that the Holy Spirit is the bond of fellowship.

For by one Spirit we were all baptized into one body,
whether Jews or Greeks, whether slaves or free, and we
were all made to drink of one Spirit.[15]

When one sings the song, "Blest Be the Tie That Binds," he is sing
Holy Spirit that binds Christians together in fellowship.

Fellowship in the church is not based upon common inter
background, common needs or common lifestyle. It is based upon the common
Spirit that dwells in every Christian.[16] The same Holy Spirit dwells in every
Christian. He is the tie that binds men of every land and language together in
Christ.

Christian fellowship is grounded in Divinity. The theological basis for
this fellowship is found in the Father, Son and Holy Spirit. God begat us as His
sons and by being born again we became a part of His family. Christ reconciled
us to God through the cross, and "in Christ" we have fellowship with all others
who have been reconciled to God. The Holy Spirit dwells in every Christian
and becomes the tie that binds us together as one. Fellowship was initiated by
Divinity and is sustained by Divinity. This fellowship is holy!

The "in Christ" fellowship is not determined by men, their institutions or
their creeds. It is decreed by God. Men only acknowledge what God has
decreed.

It is the Divine nature of this fellowship which makes it so precious, for
in it one is able to commune with God. It is the Divine nature of this fellowship
which makes it so strong. It can overcome all barriers that divide men. It is the
Divine nature of this fellowship that makes it so powerful. It provides the
strongest of motives to call one back from sin and error.

It should be observed that fellowship cannot be imposed upon an
unwilling recipient. It is a "two-way street." Two brothers might be in
fellowship with God because they are His children. By definition they would
be in fellowship with one another as brothers. This is not always the case. The
fellowship between these brothers is dependent upon their being willing to
give and receive fellowship. It takes the willingness of both parties for genuine
koinonia to exist.

Such is involved in the very meaning of the word, *koinonia*. Harry Pickup
Jr. shows this in his study of the word. Quoting from Moulton and Milligan and
giving a summary, he writes:

> "*Koinonein* is always used of active participation
> where the result depends on the cooperation of the
> receiver as well as on the action of the giver." This
> point clearly establishes that fellowship is not
> mere relationship and that it is controlled, at least
> to some extent, by the parties involved.[17]

The giver cannot impose fellowship against the will of the receiver. God has made fellowship between men possible through Christ. Men can limit this possibility by their refusal of giving and receiving fellowship.

Willingness on both the part of the giver and receiver is shown by Jesus. Reconciliation between brethren is essential before one presents his offering to God.[18] Even though fellowship "in Christ" is determined by God, it can be thwarted by men.

Triune Nature of Fellowship

It is important to understand that fellowship "in Christ" involves more than a dual relationship between God and man or a dual relationship between man and man. The relationship is triune — "God, me and my brother."

Certainly there are times when one communes with God in a vertical way, such as in private prayer. Others do not appear to be involved in this personal fellowship. Certainly there are times one enjoys the company of other Christians, when God's name is not mentioned and no sacred terms are involved. God does not appear to be involved in this fellowship. Is this correct?

No! One cannot divorce one's relationship with God from his relationship with God's other children. One cannot separate one's relationship with his brethren from his relationship with God. Fellowship involves more than a horizontal relationship with brethren or a vertical relationship with God. It involves a triangular relationship with all three.

John shows the nature of fellowship involves three things — walking in the light, fellowship with one another and the blood of Jesus.

> If we say that we have fellowship with Him and yet walk
> in the darkness, we lie and do not practice the truth; but if
> we walk in the light as He Himself is in the light, we have
> fellowship with one another, and the blood of Jesus His
> Son cleanses us from all sin.[19]

Fellowship with God is in the spiritual realm of truth and righteousness called "light." Fellowship with God involves also having "fellowship with one another." Fellowship with God is possible only through the cleansing blood of Jesus Christ.

John further expresses the triune nature of fellowship in the discussion of *agape* love. He shows that love for God and love for a brother cannot be separated.

24

If some one says, "I love God," and hates his brother, he is
a liar, for the one who does not love his brother whom he
has seen, cannot love God whom he has not seen. And this
commandment we have from Him, that the one who loves
God should love his brother also.[20]

One cannot be in fellowship with God and out of fellowship with his brother
who is in fellowship with God. God turns His face from those who refuse to
give fellowship to His other children.

Husbands are instructed to dwell with their wives according to knowledge and give honor to them"so that your prayers may not be hindered."[21] The
inference is that domestic estrangement hinders prayers to God.

Jesus Himself gave a similar instruction when speaking of the sin of anger
in the Sermon on the Mount.

If therefore you are presenting your offering at the altar,
and there remember that your brother has something
against you, leave your offering there before the altar,
and go your way, first be reconciled to your brother, and
then come and present your offering.[22]

Before one can approach God, he must seek to erase the estrangement between
himself and an offended brother. Fellowship is triangular. Fellowship with
God and fellowship with brethren go together.

The same principle applies to extending fellowship to a brother who is
out of fellowship with God. To do so is to share—have fellowship—in his evil
doing.

This principle is taught in II John. The context is that there were false
teachers circulating in the brotherhood. They were going from congregation to
congregation teaching a false doctrine and expecting brethren where they
went to support them with hospitality. John said it was wrong to give them this
hospitality because to do so was to extend fellowship to them.

Any one who goes too far and does not abide in the
teaching of Christ, does not have God; the one who abides
in the teaching, he has both the Father and the Son. If any
one comes to you and does not bring this teaching, do not
receive him into your house, and do not give him a
greeting; for the one who gives him a greeting participates
in his evil deeds.[23]

Koinonia

This passage gives fundamental teachings on the limits of fellowship. Notice four things.

First, "the teaching of Christ" is the criteria by which a false teacher is to be judged.[24]

Second, one who does not abide in the teaching of Christ has broken fellowship with God — "does not have God."

Third, those who do not abide in the teaching are not to be given hospitality because they have broken fellowship with God.

Fourth, giving hospitality to those who do not have fellowship with God compromises one's own relationship to God. To do such causes one to be a partaker in the evil deeds of the false teacher.

Fellowship with God and fellowship with His children are interconnected. They cannot be separated. One cannot have fellowship with one without the other.

Chart #1 Fellowship in Christ can be compared to a triangle. The points of the triangle are "God, me and my brother." God is the apex of the triangle. My brother and I are the horizonal points of the triangle. Genuine fellowship in Christ exists when all of the lines of the triangle are unbroken. When both my brother and I are in fellowship with God, then we are in fellowship with each other.

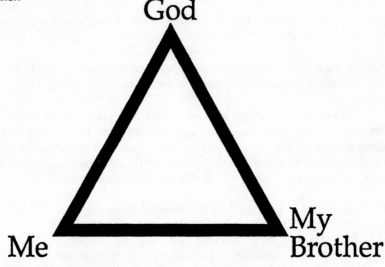

"But if we walk in the light as He Himself is in the light, we have fellowship with one another" — I John 1:7

26

Chart #2 When either my brother or I break fellowship with God, then fellowship should be broken between us. This is not based on the judgment of man; it is only a recognition of the break in fellowship that has already happened between God and one of His children. The break in fellowship between my brother and me in this case is not motivated by political interest, personal dislike or pretentious righteousness. It is motivated by and demanded because of one's loyalty to Jesus Christ.

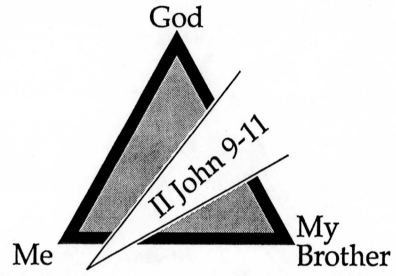

"*Any one who goes too far and does not abide in the teaching of Christ, does not have God . . . If any one comes to you and does not bring this teaching, do not receive him ...*"
— II John 9, 11

Chart #3 When one breaks fellowship with a faithful child of God, it also involves a break in fellowship with God. If a brother leaves the fellowship of God's children, it should be so recognized. Such was recommended by John concerning those who "went out from us."[25] Problems with a brother should be resolved before one approaches God in worship.[26] When a brother's name remains on the "church roll" long after he is out of fellowship with God because of neglect, error or sin, it is a farce. Such does not keep him in fellowship with God. The church must recognize what God has already done.

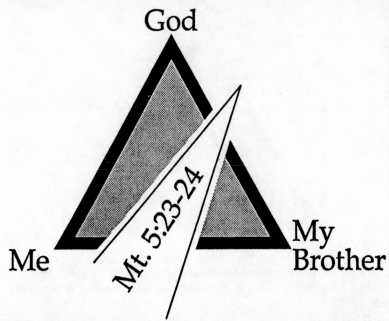

"*If therefore you are presenting your offering at the altar, and there remember that your brother has something against you, leave your offering there before the altar, and go your way, first be reconciled to your brother, and then come and present your offering.*" — Matthew 5:23-24

Endnotes

[1]Mark 1:16-18.
[2]Mark 2:14.
[3]Philippians 3:13.
[4]Philippians 3:8.
[5]Luke 14:26, 27, 33.
[6]Matthew 22:30.
[7]James 1:18.
[8]I Peter 1:23.
[9]John 3:3, 5. See also Ephesians 5:26 and Titus 3:5.
[10]Hebrews 2:9-18.
[11]Hebrews 4:15.
[12]II Corinthians 5:17-19.
[13]II Corinthians 5:21.
[14]Ephesians 2:13-16.
[15]I Corinthians 12:13.
[16]See Acts 2:38. One must not understand the Holy Spirit of God as some kind of physical thing which is poured into a Christian when he is baptized. Like God the Father, the Holy Spirit is a spiritual being without flesh and blood. He is not bound in time and space. It is beyond the understanding of man to know "how," in a metaphysical way, the Holy Spirit dwells in a Christian just as it is beyond the understanding of man to know "how" in a metaphysical way, the Word became flesh in Jesus Christ. It is sufficient on both counts to just believe the testimony of the Scriptures.
[17]Harry Pickup Jr., *The Fellowship of Jesus Christ Our Lord* (Atlanta, Georgia: Publishing Systems, Inc., 1974), p. 7.
[18]Matthew 5:24.
[19]I John 1:6-7.
[20]I John 4:20-21.
[21]I Peter 3:7.
[22]Matthew 5:23-24.
[23]II John 9-11.
[24]There are two understandings of the content of the phrase "teaching of Christ." If *to Christou* is an objective genitive, then it would refer to the teaching about Christ noted in verse 7 which denied that Jesus came in the flesh. If *to Christou* is a subjective genitive, then it would refer to the teaching from Christ or by His authority. This would include all Jesus taught and all the apostles taught by His authority.

Abraham J. Malherbe takes the former view in an article entitled, Through
the Eye of the Needle: "The Doctrine of Christ", *Restoration Quarterly* : Vol.
6:1, pp. 12-18.

J. W. Roberts, though not affirming either view, gives a good discussion of
the latter view in his book entitled, *The Letters of John* : R. B. Sweet Co., Inc.
Austin, Texas, 1968, pp. 164-164.

There is nothing in the grammar of the passage which would indicate
which of these views is correct. Whether the *to Christou* is a subjective
genitive or an objective genitive must be determined by the context. Even
the context does not resolve the problem.

If one considers the "immediate context" of only verse 7 — "those who do
not acknowledge Jesus Christ as coming in the flesh" — one would con-
clude that it was an objective genitive. John is referring to the doctrine
"about Christ." (See also I John 3:1-3; John 1:14-18.)

If one considers the "broader context" of all of II John and John's other
writings about the identity of the false teachers he is refuting, one must opt
for the subjective genitive. John is referring to the doctrine which comes by
the authority of Christ. This includes the rejection of Jesus coming in the
flesh, but much more is involved. These false teachers seemed to be
questioning the absolute nature of truth and its relationship to His word
(II John 1-4; I John 2:4-6). These false teachers seemed to be questioning the
necessity of keeping commandments (II John 4-7; I John 3:18-4:3; John
12:44-50). All three of these passages connect the humanity of Jesus — his
"coming in the flesh" — with commandment keeping or the word of Jesus
which will be the basis of final judgment.) The false teachers seemed to be
rejecting the fellowship of brethren. (They had left the fellowship — I John
2:19. They were denying the demands of fellowship by refusing to help
those in need — I John 3:16-18).

The exegesis of the passage will be determined by whether one interprets it
in its broad or immediate context. The ultimate understanding of both
interpretations do not greatly differ. The belief that Jesus came in the flesh
would certainly involve His authoritative teachings. The genuine acceptance of the teachings from Christ would certainly involve an understanding that He came in the flesh. Abraham Malherbe summarized his article

with this statement, "For John it is impossible to separate the true message about God's revelation in Christ from the person of Christ" (Op. Cit. p. 18).
[25]I John 2:19.
[26]Matthew 5:23.

Study Questions

1. Why is it important to have the basis of fellowship "grounded in Divinity"?

2. Discuss the triune nature of fellowship? How is this practical in life situations?

3. Is it possible to break fellowship with a brother and still maintain fellowship with God? If so, what are the circumstances?

4. Discuss the priority Jesus said His followers must have in their relationship with Him (Luke 14:26-27, 33).

5. Why can loyalty to fellowship in the body supercede other loyalties that one has in life?

6. Fellowship with God is possible only through the cleansing of the blood of Jesus Christ. Discuss.

7. Discuss the charts used in this lesson and give some practical evaluations for life situations.

3/New Testament Analogies

"Perhaps the strongest test of brotherly love is the willingness to confront a brother who is involved in sin or error."

The New Testament idea of "fellowship in Christ" can best be understood if one looks at it from different perspectives. It is important to understand the meanings of the words which are used to express the concept.[1] It is important to understand the theological basis the teaching stands upon.[2] It is also helpful to examine the descriptive analogies that are used in the New Testament to describe it.

Family Analogy

One of the richest analogies used to describe fellowship in the New Testament is the "family." Those involved in the fellowship are all a part of the family of God. They have been begotten by the same Father and experienced the same spiritual birth.[3] This new birth establishes a new relationship with

God by which they are both able to call Him "Abba, Father" and become identified as "heirs of God."[4] It is a tie of blood. It is not the blood tie of ethnic clan or physical family. It is the blood tie of Jesus Christ. All who are in the family of God have been cleansed by the blood of Jesus Christ.

This analogy involves other aspects of the family relationship. The discipline of trials is proof of a father's love.[5] Confidence that God will answer one's prayers is compared to the desire that a physical father has to grant the requests of his children.[6]

This analogy focuses on one's identity as God's child. As a part of the family of God, one is confident that God will deal with him as one of his children. He knows that the Father will desire the best for him, give the best to him, and expect the best of him because he is a child of God. Because of this family identity, a Christian's lifestyle is different from the world. He can expect to be misunderstood. John showed this to be true even in the first century.

> See how great a love the Father has bestowed upon us, that
> we should be called children of God; and such we are. For
> this reason the world does not know us, because it did not
> know Him... By this the children of God and the children
> of the devil are obvious; any one who does not practice
> righteousness is not of God, nor the one who does not love
> his brother.[7]

This identity in God's family keeps one from feeling alone in the world. It gives him confidence that God cares about his needs. It keeps him from letting the world's values absorb his life.[8]

Very much involved in this family analogy is the idea of the brotherhood with all of God's children. If God is the Father, then all of His children are brothers and sisters. If one identifies with the Father, he also identifies with His children. The term "brother" describes this relationship. It is used some 230 times in the New Testament.

The descriptive term "brother" is often used in the New Testament to describe the relationship involved in Christian fellowship.

This term reflects a relationship of equality with all others who are God's children. Jesus condemned the scribes and Pharisees because of their desire to be exalted above others and taught that this must not be true of His disciples.

> But do not be called Rabbi; for One is your Teacher, and
> you are all brothers.[9]

The term reflects a relationship of mutual concern. There is a spiritual family tie that binds all of God's children together in brotherly love. This tie is grounded in one being born again and finds expression in a heart felt love.

> Since you have in obedience to the truth purified your
> souls for a sincere love of the brethren, fervently love
> one another from the heart, for you have been born again
> not of seed which is perishible but imperishable, that is,
> through the living and abiding word of God.[10]

This mutual concern overcomes strife. One is able to overlook weaknesses and bear with agitation because the concern for the family is greater than personal concerns. This aspect of family love is seen in Abraham's offering the best pasture land to his nephew Lot in order to keep strife from continuing between their herdsmen.

> Please let there be no strife between you and me, nor
> between my herdsmen and your herdsmen, for we are
> brothers. Is not the whole land before you? Please
> separate from me: If to the left, then I will go to the right;
> or if to the right, then I will go to the left.[11]

Concern for brotherhood outweighed any personal rights or selfish desires.
This mutual concern of the family causes all who are children of God to treat one another as special people. They give preferential treatment to one another because of the family ties. They are spiritual kinfolk. Paul shows this to be the case even in the explosive social relationship of master and slave.

> And let those who have believers as their masters not
> be disrespectful to them because they are brethren, but
> let them serve them all the more, because those who
> partake of the benefit are believers and beloved.[12]

The relationship of being a brother in God's family overcomes all social, economic and ethnic barriers which exist in the world. The priority relationship is always that of spiritual brotherhood.
This mutual concern extends to benevolent help for the needy in God's family. Such is witnessed at the very beginning of the church.

And all those who had believed were together and had
all things in common; and they began selling their
property and possessions, and were sharing them with
all, as anyone might have need.[13]

Being a part of the family of God involves a sharing of resources with other
members of the family who are in need. Such a family concern with the
brethren cannot be separated from one's relationship with God.

We know love by this, that He laid down His life for us;
and we ought to lay down our lives for the brethren.
But whoever has the world's goods, and beholds his
brother in need and closes his heart against him, how
does the love of God abide in him?[14]

This mutual concern also involves itself in the spiritual welfare of all who are
in God's family. If brotherly love demands concern for the needs of the body,
much more does it demand concern for the needs of the soul. It is totally
contrary to brotherly love for one to stand by in passive silence while his
brother becomes involved in sin or dies of spiritual indifference. The bonds of
brotherhood make such intolerable. Both Paul and James challenge all of God's
children to be concerned for any brother who is overcome in sin.

Brethren, even if a man is caught in any tresspass, you
who are spiritual restore such a one in a spirit of
gentleness; looking to yourself, lest you too be tempted.[15]

My brethren, if any among you strays from the truth, and
one turns him back; let him know that he who turns a
sinner from the error of his way will save his soul from
death, and will cover a multitude of sins.[16]

Perhaps the strongest test of brotherly love is the willingness to confront a
brother who is involved in sin or error. If one really values the relationships of
the family of God, he will care enough to correct his brother.

The main lesson that Jesus taught in the parable of the prodigal son is
often missed. The chief point that Jesus made in the parable was not so much
the shameful rebellion of the younger son or the unfailing love of the father. It
was rather the cold and uncaring heart of the elder brother.

36

The context of the parable was the criticism that the scribes and Pharisees gave about Jesus eating with tax collectors and sinners.[17] His response to them was a parable which exposed the hard and selfish heart of one who refused to show compassion to his penitent brother who came back to the father's house. The very words of the elder brother show an attitude totally incompatible to genuine brotherhood.

> But he answered and said to his father, "Look! For so
> many years I have been serving you, and I have never
> neglected a command of yours; and yet you have never
> given me a kid, that I might be merry with my friends;
> but when this son of yours came, who has devoured
> your wealth with harlots, you killed the fattened calf
> for him.[18]

The elder brother's refusal to even call the prodigal son a brother reflected the hardness of his heart. Even though he remained in the Father's house, he was still not a part of the family. He was unwilling to extend fellowship to his returning brother.

A song by Lanny Wolfe expresses the depth of brotherhood in the family of God.[19]

> We're part of the family
> That's been born again
> Part of the family
> Whose love knows no end
> For Jesus has saved us
> And made us His own
> Now we're part of the family
> That's on its way home
>
> When a brother meets sorrow
> We all feel his grief
> When he's passed thru the valley
> We all feel relief
> Together in sunshine
> Together in rain
> Together in victory
> Thru His precious name

And sometimes we laugh together,
Sometimes we cry;
Sometimes we share together
Heartaches and sighs
Sometimes we dream together
Of how it will be
When we all get to heaven
God's Family

Body Analogy

The human body is used as an analogy for understanding fellowship in the writings of Paul. At least fifteen different passages in the New Testament use some aspect of the human body to describe fellowship interactions in the church.[20]

Three things are reflected in the use of the body analogy. First, it shows the relationship of the body to its head, Jesus Christ. Second, it shows the interdependence of the different members of the body on one another. Third, it shows the oneness of the body even in the diversity of its members.

Jesus is the head of the body — the church. This is the emphasis of the body analogy in both Ephesians and Colossians.[21] The authority of Christ is shown by Jesus being the "head" of the body — the church. It is this headship which involves the church's submission to Christ. Just as the head of the physical body directs the activity of all of its members, so Christ directs the activities of all of the members of His body — the church.

The interdependence of the members of the church on one another is reflected in the body analogy.[22] The members of the physical body are different from one another and each have different functions. This does not make for jealousy, competition and confusion. The different members complement one another and bring strength out of diversity.

This idea is particularly clear in Paul's correction of the abuse of spiritual gifts at Corinth. In the context of showing that those who had showy spiritual gifts were no better than those who had none, he writes:

And the eye cannot say to the hand, "I have no need of
you"; or again the head to the feet, "I have no need of you."
On the contrary, it is much truer that the members of the
body which seem to be weaker are necessary;[23]

38

In the context of showing that those who did not possess showy spiritual gifts were important, he writes:

> If the foot should say, "Because I am not a hand, I am not
> a part of the body," it is not for this reason any the less
> a part of the body. And if the ear should say, "Because I
> am not an eye, I am not a part of the body," it is not for
> this reason any the less a part of the body. If the whole
> body were an eye, where would the hearing be? If the
> whole were hearing, where would the sense of smell be?
> But now God has placed the members, each one of them,
> in the body, just as He desired.[24]

The body analogy shows that the least gifted member is important to the body and the most glamorously gifted members need the other members. No one in Christ's body — the church — can feel that they do not need others. No one can feel that they are unnecessary.

This knowledge that — just as the members of the physical body depend on each other, so members of the church depend on each other — adds a very important dimension to fellowship in Christ. This understanding caused Paul to exhort the Corinthians to really care for one another.

> ...that there should be no division in the body, but
> that the members should have the same care for one
> another. And if one member suffers, all the members
> suffer with it; if one member is honored, all the
> members rejoice with it. Now you are Christ's body,
> and individually members of it.[25]

What affects one member of the body, affects every other member and even the Head of the body, Jesus Christ.[26] The bonds of fellowship tie together every individual member of the church with one another and with Jesus the Head.

The oneness of the church in the midst of individual diversity is reflected in the body analogy. Six out of the fifteen passages describing the church as the body of Christ use the term "one body." Ethnic differences, economic barriers, social divisions and variation of abilities do not divide the body. Such diversity enhances its unity.

In the context of discussing the diversity of gifts in the church at Rome, Paul gives the following instruction:

For just as we have many members in one body and
all the members do not have the same function, so we,
who are many, are one body in Christ, and individually
members one of another. And since we have gifts that
differ according to the grace given to us, let each
exercise them accordingly.[27]

Diversity gives opportunity for mutual service, not selfish exaltation or shameful humiliation. Since it is by God's grace that gifts are given, no one can glory in himself. Glory is given to God as each individual ministers his gift for the benefit of the total body.

The theological basis of fellowship between men who were formerly separated by human barriers is explained under the body analogy. In the context of showing that Jews and Gentiles are united in Christ, Paul writes:

But now in Christ Jesus you who formerly were far off
have been brought near by the blood of Christ. For He
Himself is our peace, who made both groups into one,
and broke down the barrier of the dividing wall, by
abolishing in His flesh the enmity, which is the Law
of commandments contained in ordinances, that in
Himself He might make the two into one new man,
thus establishing peace, and might reconcile them both
in one body to God through the cross.[28]

The body analogy shows not only the fellowship with God through the cross but also fellowship between all men who are "in Christ."

One Anotherness

The phrase "one another" is not an analogy but is considered at this place in the discussion because it reflects so well some important dimensions of fellowship in Christ.

Lanelle Waters' little book entitled *"The One Another Way,"* lists nearly one hundred different New Testament passages which refer to the "one anotherness" of fellowship.[29] These passages are then listed under twenty-seven different categories. Each of these categories reflects the interaction that needs to exist in the fellowship of the church. Some of the listings are as follows:

Care for one another...
Teach and admonish one another...
Bear one another's burdens...
Admonish one another...
Serving one another...
Encourage one another...
Be kind to one another...
Give preference to one another...
Be hospitable to one another...
Be subject to one another...
Love one another...
Be at peace with one another...
Forgive one another...
Pray for one another...
Accept one another...
Be of the same mind toward one another...

Certainly these fellowship exhortations from the scriptures reflect the responsibility that rests upon those who are "in the fellowship." Fellowship in Christ is not merely something that one passively receives from others. It involves active participation. It involves sharing. It involves community.

The term "one another" describes a mutual and reciprocal responsibility which those involved in the "in Christ" fellowship have in their relationships.[30] It is not duty but caring concern which motivates the actions of this relationship.

One can no more have fellowship without personal involvement than he can "teeter totter" by himself.

Endnotes

[1]See Chapter I.
[2]See Chapter II.
[3]See pages 12-13.
[4]Romans 8:14-17; Galatians 4:6,7.
[5]Hebrews 12:1-13.
[6]Matthew 7:7-12.
[7]I John 3:1, 10.
[8]I John 2:15-17.

⁹Matthew 23:8.
¹⁰I Peter 1:22-23.
¹¹Genesis 13:8-9.
¹²I Timothy 6:2.
¹³Acts 2:44-45.
¹⁴I John 3:16-17.
¹⁵Galatians 6:1.
¹⁶James 5:19-20.
¹⁷Luke 15:1-2.
¹⁸Luke 15:29-30.
¹⁹Used by permission of the Lanny Wolfe Music Co. of Nashville, Tennessee.
²⁰Romans 12:4; I Corinthians 10:16-17; 11:29; 12:12-27; Ephesians 1:22-23; 2:16; 3:6; 4:4; 4:11-16; 5:23; Colossians 1:18; 1:24; 2:19; 3:15; Hebrews 13:3. Six of these fifteen passages refer to the "oneness" of the body. Ephesians has the "body" analogy in every chapter.
²¹Ephesians 1:22-23; 5:23-24; Colossians 1:18, 24; 2:19.
²²Romans 12:4-8; I Corinthians 12:12-27; Ephesians 4:11-16.
²³I Corinthians 12:21-22.
²⁴I Corinthians 12:16-19.
²⁵I Corinthians 12:25-27.
²⁶Matthew 25:40; I Corinthians 8:12.
²⁷Romans 12:4-6.
²⁸Ephesians 2:13-16.
²⁹Lanelle Waters, *The One Another Way* (Gainsville, Florida: Crossroads Publications, 1979).
³⁰Gene A. Getz, *Building Up One Another* (Wheaton, Illinois: Victor Books, 1979). This book is written around the "one another" relationships in the New Testament.

Study Questions

1. Discuss what it means to be a family (in the church).

2. How is the "body analogy" related to function within the body of Christ?

3. How are we to practice our Christianity toward "one another" and how is this to be understood on a day-to-day basis?

4. Discuss how concern for brotherhood can outweigh any personal rights or selfish desires for an individual.

5. Discuss how mutual concern involves itself in the spiritual welfare of all who are in God's family.

6. What is the main lesson that Jesus taught in the parable of the prodigal son?

7. Discuss how we are all different members but each of the same body. How does this relate to different functions?

8. Give examples of how what affects one member of the body, affects every other member and even the head, Jesus Christ.

4/ The New Testament Practice of Fellowship

"Never, never does one hear of an inspired man speaking in a derogatory way of either the church or the brotherhood."

"...the threat of denying fellowship is the strongest tool the church has in breaking the bondage that the devil has over a fellow Christian."

If one is to understand the New Testament teachings on "fellowship in Christ," a number of things must be done.

Words must be defined. The theological basis upon which a teaching rests must be studied. Analogies used to describe fellowship in the New Testament must be examined.

One of the the best means of understanding the New Testament teachings of fellowship is to examine the practices of the early church. One can better understand a tree by examining the fruit it produces. One can better understand fellowship by examining the fellowship practices of the New Testament church.

Fellowship Identity

Early Christians felt a strong sense of identity in the fellowship of the church. This identity involved both Christ and the church.

In the new birth one experienced a new identity. His old identity was lost. It was like putting off old dirty clothes.[1] It was like breaking the chains of bondage.[2] It was a beginning of a new life of holiness.[3] Paul described the passing away of the old identity and finding a new identity in Christ.

> Therefore if any man is in Christ, he is a new creature;
> the old things passed away; behold, new things have
> come.[4]

This new identity finds its basis in one's relationship to Jesus Christ.

One identifies with Jesus' death in dying to sin. One identifies with Jesus' burial in the tomb at his baptism. One identifies with Jesus' resurrection when he arises from the waters of baptism a "new creature."[5] This newness of life and identity is described by Paul in his own life.

> I have been crucified with Christ; and it is no longer I
> who live, but Christ lives in me; and the life which I now
> live in the flesh I live by faith in the Son of God, who
> loved me, and delivered Himself up for me.[6]

Paul's old identity was lost and his new identity found when he became a Christian. His new identity was grounded in his relationship to Christ. Hans Kung describes this new identity.

> Baptism is therefore not only a condition but also a
> guarantee of being made a part of the Church. Man is
> removed from the loneliness of his own ego, and finds
> a home in community. On the basis of this sign he can
> be sure and proud of his membership.[7]

This identity with Christ also causes one to be identified with all others who find a new identity in Christ. This is the basis of fellowship in the church. This common identity is described by fellowship words in the early church. In the context of persecution, it is said of Christians:

...you endured a great conflict of sufferings, partly,
by being made a public spectacle through reproaches and
tribulations, and partly by becoming sharers with those
who were so treated. For you showed sympathy to the
prisoners, and accepted joyfully the seizure of your
property.[8]

This identity of Christians with one another resulted in a feeling of "one for all and all for one." Any idea of private communion with Christ without involving active participation in the life of the church is totally foreign to the New Testament. What happened to one was experienced by all. Paul described this under the analogy of the church being a body.

And if one member suffers, all the members suffer with
it; if one member is honored, all the members rejoice
with it. Now you are Christ's body, and individually
members of it.[9]

The early Christians were not to be ashamed of being identified in this fellowship. They were to offer no apologies. They were not to be intimidated by threats. They were rather to glory in the opportunity of being identified as Christians, even if it meant suffering.

If you are reviled for the name of Christ, you are
blessed, because the Spirit of glory and of God rests
upon you. By no means let any of you suffer as a murderer,
or thief, or evildoer, or troublesome meddler; but if
anyone suffers as a Christian, let him not feel ashamed,
but in that name let him glorify God.[10]

Christians are not to be ashamed of their identity with either Christ or the church. They stand out as different[11] and stand up for the name of Christ in all situations.[12] One reads in the New Testament of members of the church who sin, rebel and teach false doctrine. They are rebuked and warned. Never, never does one hear of an inspired man speaking in a derogatory way of either the church or the brotherhood. They did not see themselves as judges above the church but gloried in being identified with the church. They really "loved the brotherhood."[13]

Expressions of Fellowship

A number of the practices of the early church were very clear expressions of fellowship in Christ. Fellowship was more than something to talk about; it was also something to be experienced in the life of the church. When the fellowship aspect of these practices would be neglected or perverted, an apostolic correction was forthcoming.

The Lord's Supper was one of the practices of the church that involved fellowship. Such was a part of its very nature. The Lord's Supper is sometimes called "communion" because this term was used in the King James Version to describe it.

> The cup of blessing which we bless, is it not the
> communion of the blood of Christ? The bread which we
> break, is it not the communion of the body of Christ?[14]

In the Lord's Supper, one is having communion or fellowship with both Jesus and all of His followers. Jesus Himself said when He instituted the Lord's Supper:

> I will not drink of this fruit of the vine from now on
> until that day when I drink it new with you in My Father's
> kingdom.[15]

Jesus was teaching that the Lord's Supper was a "communal meal" in which He would share with His disciples in the coming kingdom.

The Lord's Supper is also a communion with other Christians. Not only is it a "sharing with Christ," but it is also a "sharing with one another." In the context of correcting the abuse of the Lord's Supper, Paul rebukes the Corinthians because they were not waiting for one another or sharing with one another.[16] There were divisions in the fellowship of the church. This made the correct observance of the Lord's Supper impossible.

> For, in the first place, when you come together as a
> church, I hear that divisions exist among you...
> Therefore when you meet together, it is not to eat the
> Lord's Supper.[17]

Paul perhaps even makes a play on words to show the twofold nature of the communion in the Lord's Supper. He seems to refer to the "body" in verse 27 as being the unleavened bread used in the Lord's Supper. In verse 29 he seems to refer to the "body" as being the church. Both bodies are involved. In the Lord's Supper one communes with both the body of Jesus that was crucified and the body of His church.

The observance of the Lord's Supper is a practice that expresses the triune fellowship in Christ. In it there is fellowship with Christ and one another in the church.

The Christian assembly was a practice that expressed fellowship in Christ. Luke describes the practice soon after Pentecost:

> And all those who had believed were together, and had
> all things in common;... And day by day continuing
> with one mind in the temple, and breaking bread from
> house to house, they were taking their meals together
> with gladness and sincerity of heart.[18]

Early Christians came together to observe the Lord's Supper as an expression of fellowship.[19]

They met together to edify one another through singing and teaching. All things were to be done for edification.[20] Concern for one another in the fellowship was essential. Their assembly was more than "Sunday tolerance" of one another. It was a deep, abiding love that motivated Christians to want to be with one another.

They met together as a body to exercise discipline. In fellowship with one another they withdrew fellowship from a brother who was immoral. This is the instruction given by Paul.

> In the name of our Lord Jesus, when you are assembled,
> and I with you in spirit, with the power of our Lord Jesus,
> I have decided to deliver such a one to Satan for the
> destruction of his flesh, that his spirit may be saved in
> the day of the Lord Jesus.[21]

It was the wrongful denial of fellowship in the assembly of Christians which caused Paul to rebuke Peter to his face at Antioch.

For prior to the coming of certain men from James, he
used to eat with the Gentiles; but when they came,
he began to withdraw and hold himself aloof, fearing
the party of the circumcision.[22]

Denial of fellowship because of party lines is hypocritical. When such is
practiced in the assembly of Christians, it needs to be rebuked.

The contribution which Christians give to support the needy[23] and
preach the Gospel[24] is an expression of fellowship. In fact, the term *koinonia* ,
used by Paul to refer to the collection taken up by the church at Corinth, is
translated "contribution" in most English texts.[25]

The fellowship idea is to be seen in those incidents in the early church
when they "had all things in common."[26]

The fellowship idea is found in Paul's description of the contribution that
was taken by the churches of Macedonia.

...that in great ordeal of affliction their abundance of
joy and their deep poverty overflowed in the wealth of
their liberality. For I testify that according to their
ability, and beyond their ability they gave of their own
accord, begging us with much entreaty for the favor of
participation in the support of the saints.[27]

One of the clearest passages expressing the fellowship content of the contribu-
tion is found in Romans. In the context of reporting his plans of traveling to
Jerusalem with a contribution from the churches of Macedonia and Achaia,
Paul shows that fellowship flows both ways between Jews and Gentiles. Just
as the Jews shared spiritual things in preaching the Gospel to the Gentiles, the
Gentiles shared physical things by sending a contribution to the Jews.

For Macedonia and Achaia have been pleased to make a
contribution for the poor among the saints in Jerusalem.
Yes, they were pleased to do so, and they are indebted
to them. For if the Gentiles have shared in their spiritual
things, they are indebted to minister to them also in
material things.[28]

The contributions collected by the churches were an expression of fellowship.
In these contributions they were able to share with brethren who were in

physical need and share in preaching the Gospel by supporting those who did the preaching. It was one of the practices that bound Christians together into the oneness of fellowship.

The Christian practice of fellowship through sharing is well attested to in post-biblical sources. The early church was recognized by its pagan neighbors as practicing a fellowship of sharing. Tertullian wrote:

> It is our care for the helpless, our practice of
> loving kindness, that brands us in the eyes of many of
> our opponents. "Only look," they say, "look how they
> love one another... Look how they are prepared to
> die for one another."[29]

Justin Martyr in his description of early Christian worship wrote of the practice and purpose of the contribution.

> Those who are well-to-do and willing, give as they
> choose, each as he himself purposes; the collection is
> then deposited with the president, who succours
> orphans, widows, those who are in want owing to
> sickness or any other cause, those who are in prison,
> and strangers who are on a journey.[30]

Christian hospitality is an expression of fellowship. Christians who were on mission journeys or business journeys enjoyed the hospitality of Christians in whose city they dwelt. This provided protection, lodging and food when one was away from home. Particularly was this needed in a time when there were not public accommodations for travelers. This hospitality was an expression of fellowship in Christ.

Of special significance in Christian hospitality was the sharing of a meal. More was involved than satisfying hunger and obtaining nourishment. There was a communal aspect of eating together.

The early Christians' love feasts were an expression of this fellowship. Both Peter and Jude warned against allowing false teachers to participate in their love feasts. They were "stains and blemishes" which defiled the sanctity of Christian fellowship.[31]

The fellowship ties of sharing a common meal together are reflected in the way Jesus expressed the betrayal of Judas. At the last supper Jesus told His disciples of His coming betrayal. He was very troubled in spirit because this betrayal would come from one of the twelve He had chosen. To express the magnitude of this betrayal He quoted from the Psalms.

> Even my close friend, in whom I trusted, who ate my
> bread, has lifted up his heel against me.[32]

Judas' betrayal was turning away from a friend. It was also a breaking of the table fellowship that had just been experienced in the last supper. It is contradictory action to "share in a meal" with a friend and then betray him. Sharing a meal together, participating in the love feasts, and partaking of the Lord's Supper were all expressions of Christian fellowship.

In the first century church, Christian teachers would travel from place to place in their work. They expected and received hospitality from brethren with whom they worked. Two things began to complicate this arrangement by the close of the New Testament period. First, false teachers arose. Second, this fellowship was abused by teachers who demanded hospitality without working.

The solution to the first problem is found in the New Testament text. John writes that the church is not to receive a teacher and give him hospitality if his doctrine is not according to the teaching of Christ:

> If any one comes to you and does not bring this teaching,
> do not receive him into your house, and do not give him
> a greeting; for the one who gives him a greeting
> participates in his evil deeds.[33]

The denial of fellowship to a false teacher is not merely an act of convenience; it is a demand of fellowship. Giving support to a false teacher is to have fellowship with him in his evil work.

The solution to the second problem is found in a principle established for disciplining those who refused to work. In the context of dealing with lazy brethren who expected to be supported by the church in their slothful lifestyle, Paul gave a plain rule:

> For even when we were with you, we used to give you
> this order: If anyone will not work, neither let him eat.
> For we hear that some among you are leading an
> undisciplined life, doing no work at all, but acting like
> busybodies. Now such persons we command and exhort
> in the Lord Jesus Christ to work in quiet fashion and eat
> their own bread.[34]

A second century document, *The Didache*, gave added counsel on how to keep Christian hospitality from being abused:

> Now about apostles and prophets: Act in line with the
> gospel precept. Welcome every apostle on arriving, as
> if he were the Lord. But he must not stay beyond one
> day. In case of necessity, however, the next day too.
> If he stays three days, he is a false prophet. On departing,
> an apostle must not accept anything save sufficient food
> to carry him till his next lodging. If he asks for money,
> he is a false prophet...

> Everyone "who comes" to you "in the name of the Lord"
> must be welcomed. Afterward, when you have tested him,
> you will find out about him, for you have insight into
> right and wrong. If it is a traveler who arrives, help him
> all you can, but he must not stay with you more than
> two days, or, if necessary, three. If he wants to settle
> with you and is an artisan, he must work for his living.[35]

Showing hospitality is a part of Christian fellowship. Peter said it is to be shown without complaint.[36] In Hebrews it is identified as being a part of brotherly love and must be given even to those who are in prison.

> Let love of the brethren continue. Do not neglect to show
> hospitality to strangers, for by this some have
> entertained angels without knowing it. Remember the
> prisoners, as though in prison with them; and those
> who are ill-treated, since you yourselves also are in
> the body .[37]

Hospitality is to be extended to strangers and prisoners. Fellowship is expressed as the helper becomes united with the ones who are being helped.

Fellowship As a Motivation

Fellowship in Christ is precious to a Christian. It is warm and rich. It fills his need to love and be loved. It is the motivation for service and sacrifice. It is the sphere in which one receives strength from others to mature in Christ. Such a fellowship is valuable and Christians must protect it with all of their being.

Anything that would weaken this fellowship should be shunned. Anything that would break this fellowship should be feared. Anything that would hinder this fellowship should be avoided.

The great value that a Christian places on this fellowship makes it an effective means of correcting sin and error. The possibility of losing this fellowship is used by writers of the New Testament to call Christians back to right conduct. Fellowship is a strong motivation for righteousness.

In dealing with the problem of Christians who were participating in idol worship, Paul used the idea of fellowship to call them back to the Lord. Paul recognized that an idol was not really a god and that the sacrifices made to idols were not of spiritual value. The participation in such worship to idols, however, compromised the fellowship the Christians had with the Lord.

> What do I mean then? That a thing sacrificed to idols is
> anything, or that an idol is anything? No; but I say that
> the things which the Gentiles sacrifice, they sacrifice to
> demons, and not to God; and I do not want you to become
> sharers in demons. You cannot drink the cup of the Lord,
> and the cup of demons; you cannot partake of the table
> of the Lord, and the table of demons.[38]

Idolatry is incompatible with Christians because it compromises their fellowship with God and the church.

In dealing with the problem of the abuse of tongues in the Corinthian church, Paul used the idea of fellowship again. Speaking in languages which no one understood did not complement the fellowship. It fact, it was destructive to the fellowship.

Those who possessed the showy gift of languages were exalted in pride and felt they did not need the fellowship.[39] Those who did not possess gifts felt they were so inferior that they were not a part of the fellowship.[40]

Those who possessed the showy gift of languages gloried in the exercise of the gift. Such activity was meaningless without love.[41] Love involves a relationship with one another in the fellowship of the church. If that is neglected then all of the gifts are for naught.

Those who possessed the showy gift of languages were not concerned with being understood by the rest of the congregation. Paul shows that gifts without understanding are useless and that the use of gifts in which the church is not edified is wrong.[42]

54

In dealing with the problem of an immoral brother at Corinth, Paul used the ties of fellowship in a most forceful way. He told the church to deny fellowship to the immoral brother until he repents. This action presupposes that the ties of fellowship must have been strong for this to be effective in bringing about repentance. The language is forceful and clear.

> ...that the one who has done this deed might be
> removed from your midst... deliver such a one to
> Satan... clean out the old leaven... not even to
> eat with such a one... Remove the wicked man from
> among yourselves.[43]

The discipline exercised by the church at Corinth involving the immoral brother must have been effective. He repented. When Paul wrote II Corinthians, he told them to receive the brother back into their fellowship.

> Sufficient for such a one is this punishment which
> was inflicted by the majority, so that on the contrary
> you should rather forgive and comfort him, lest
> somehow such a one be overwhelmed by excessive
> sorrow.[44]

It would seem that the threat of denying fellowship is the strongest tool the church has in breaking the bondage that the devil has over a fellow Christian.

Fellowship in Christ is precious. With this fellowship comes all kinds of spiritual support, physical help and personal identity. To be denied this fellowship, after it has been known, is a powerful force for righteousness.

This fellowship in Christ is reflected in every aspect of New Testament Christianity. The practices of worship, benevolence and hospitality are entwined with the idea of fellowship. Most of the problems that plagued the New Testament church were involved in some aspect of fellowship. Certainly one's identity as a Christian cannot be separated from his fellowship with Christ in the church.

Endnotes

[1]Colossians 3:8.
[2]Romans 6:18-22.

[3]I Corinthians 6:11.
[4]II Corinthians 5:17.
[5]Romans 6:3-4.
[6]Galatians 2:20.
[7]Hans Kung, *The Church* (New York: Sheed and Ward, 1967), p. 210.
[8]Hebrews 10:32-34.
[9]I Corinthians 12:26-27.
[10]I Peter 4:14-16.
[11]I Peter 4:4.
[12]Acts 4:9-12.
[13]I Peter 2:17.
[14]I Corinthians 10:16 in the KJV. The word translated "communion" is *koinonia* . It is translated "sharing" in the NASB.
[15]Matthew 26:29.
[16]I Corinthians 11:21-22, 33.
[17]I Corinthians 11:18, 20.
[18]Acts 2:44, 46.
[19]Acts 20:7; I Corinthians 11:17-22.
[20]I Corinthians 14:26.
[21]I Corinthians 5:4-5.
[22]Galatians 2:12.
[23]I Corinthians 16:1-2.
[24]Philippians 4:14-15.
[25]II Corinthians 9:13.
[26]Acts 2:44; 4:32. The word translated "common" is *koina* — which involves fellowship.
[27]II Corinthians 8:2-4. The word translated "participation" is *koinonia* — which involves fellowship.
[28]Romans 15:26-27.
[29]Tertullian, *Apology* , xxxix.
[30]Justin Martyr, c, lxvii.
[31]II Peter 2:13; Jude 12.
[32]Psalms 41:9 as quoted in John 13:18.
[33]II John 10-11. The word translated "participates" is *koinoneo* — a fellowship word.
[34]II Thessalonians 3:10-12.
[35]*The Didache*, 11:3-6; 12:1-3.
[36]I Peter 4:9.
[37]Hebrews 13:1-3.

[38]I Corinthians 10:19-22.
[39]I Corinthians 12:21-22.
[40]I Corinthians 12:15-19.
[41]I Corinthians 13:1-3.
[42]I Corinthians 14:14-16; 26-36.
[43]I Corinthians 5:2, 5, 7, 11, 13.
[44]II Corinthians 2:6-7.

Study Questions

1. Discuss various ways "fellowship" is expressed in the New Testament community of believers.

2. Discuss "fellowship identity" in relationship to (a) Christ, and (b) the Church.

3. Discuss Christian identity with one another as expressed in the phrase "one for all and all for one."

4. Discuss how the Lord's Supper is related to fellowship not only with Jesus but with one another.

5. How is the contribution related to fellowship?

6. Discuss the sharing of a common meal and fellowship.

7. How is fellowship affected when one brother is exalted over another?

8. How are we to handle immorality within the body? How does this relate to fellowship?

Section 2
The Scope of Fellowship

Section I was a study of the nature of fellowship in Christ. Definitions of words and meaning of analogies used in the New Testament were examined. The theological basis was established, along with the implications of fellowship in the practices of the New Testament church.

Section II is a study of the scope of fellowship in Christ. This section will involve a study of the basis by which one may know who is included in the fellowship and who must be excluded from the fellowship in Christ. The devil has sought to counterfeit true "in Christ" fellowship. On the one hand he has tried to narrow it down to the culture and traditions of men. On the other hand he has tried to make it so broad and subjective that it has no meaning at all. Attitudes that create barriers to fellowship will also be examined.

Koinonia

Problems resulting from misunderstanding the scope of fellowship have been the major sources of tension within the historical Restoration Movement in the United States.

Around the beginning of the nineteenth century in the United States, different denominational parties claiming to follow Jesus Christ were warring with one another. Most of the nation was in total unbelief. It became evident to certain religious leaders that such was not the will of God. They recalled the axiom quoted by Jesus, "A kingdom divided against itself cannot stand."[1] They bemoaned the unanswered prayer of Jesus that His followers be one in order that the world might believe.[2]

With these motivations, a religious revival began. It sought the conversion of the world and the unity of believers. These were not two goals — but merely two aspects of the same goal. Alexander Campbell, one of the most popular leaders of the movement, wrote thus:

1st. Nothing is essential to the conversion of the world but the union and co-operation of Christians.

2nd. Nothing is essential to the union of Christians but the Apostles' teaching and testimony.

Or does he choose to express the plan of the Self-Existent in other words? Then he may change the order, and say —

1st. The testimony of the Apostles is the only and all-sufficient means of uniting all Christians.

2nd. The union of Christians with the Apostles' testimony is all-sufficient and alone sufficient to the conversion of the world.[3]

The conversion of the world could only come through unity of Christians — in fellowship. The unity of Christians — in fellowship — could only come through returning to the Scriptures. Unity and restoration were not two separate goals, but two aspects of the same goal.

Campbell understood, and rightly so, that division was based upon the misunderstanding of the true character of revelation. He understood revelation had nothing to do with opinions or abstract reasonings, "for it is founded wholly and entirely upon facts."[4]

Unity — fellowship — can be accomplished only if there is a substitution of:

The Bible for all human creeds
Facts for definitions
Things for words
Faith for speculation
Unity of the faith for unity of opinion
Positive commandments of God for human legislation and
   tradition
Piety for ceremony
Morality for partisan zeal
Practice of religion for the mere profession of it.[5]

Campbell understood that unity — fellowship — could not be based upon pious sentimentality or the opinions of scholasticism. Such bases of fellowship are changing and contradictory. Unity — fellowship — could only be established upon objective criteria.

Endnotes

[1]Matthew 12:25.
[2]John 17:21.
[3]Alexander Campbell, *The Christian System* (Cincinnati: Standard Publishing Co., n. d.), p. 87.
[4]op. cit. p. 89.
[5]op. cit. p. 90.

5/ The Standards of Fellowship

"Fellowship in Christ has never been broken by anything the Bible teaches."

"Paul always spoke of the church in endearing terms — so do all of those who love Jesus today."

Divinely Decreed Fellowship

The basis of fellowship in Christ is determined by God and not man. A Christian does not decide whom he wants to include in fellowship and whom he wants to exclude from fellowship. He only recognizes what God has already determined. It is not a matter left to the will of man. It is rather a submission to the will of God. One does not choose his brother. He only recognizes one as a brother because he is one of God's children.

Horizontal fellowship between children of God is only possible because of the vertical fellowship that exists between God and each one of His children. If one is in fellowship with God, then by definition, he is in fellowship with all of God's children. If one is not in fellowship with God, then all of the human decrees, compromises and sanctions of men will not make it so.

Fellowship in Christ is not something obtained by gushy emotionalism, political compromise or legislation of men. It can only be accomplished by Divine allegiance. Warm emotions are the result of fellowship, not the cause of it. Politics and legislation deal with laws and institutions which restrain men, not with the spirit by which free men are drawn together. Submissive loyalty to Christ is the only criterion for fellowship in the church.

Fellowship in Christ is like a triangle. God is the apex of the triangle. My brother and I are the horizontal points of the triangle.[1] When any line of the triangle is broken, it automatically breaks another line of the triangle.[2]

God breaks fellowship with us when we break fellowship with a brother who remains in His fellowship. Brothers break fellowship with us when we break fellowship with God.

Results of a Divinely Decreed Fellowship

Seven things follow when one understands that fellowship in Christ has been established by Divine decree.

First, there will be caution in drawing lines of fellowship based on ethnic differences, party loyalties and private opinions. Those who insist on drawing such lines should be opposed and condemned in the same way that Paul rebuked Peter at Antioch.[3]

Second, there will be zeal to surrender human innovations which break fellowship between brethren and bring estrangement from God. The desire to erase the barriers that exist between brethren will have priority even over worship that is offered to God. Sacrifices of worship will be left "at the altar" and "reconcilation with an estranged brother" will take place before it is offered.[4]

Third, there will be a concerted effort to restore to the fellowship those brothers who have drifted away through negligence and indifference. If they refuse to be recalled, they will be recognized as being "out of fellowship" because "they went out from us."[5]

Fourth, there will be discipline administered to those who have broken fellowship with God through sin, error and rebellion. The motivation for such action will not be malicious anger but brotherly love. The basis for such action will not be personal judgement but Divine allegiance.

Fifth, there will be a renewed emphasis upon the building and maintaining of a warm, genuine and spiritual fellowship in Christ in every congregation. The strength of this fellowship will be so great that it will bind brothers together in love and cause them to open their hearts and hands to serve one another.

Sixth, there will be extensive efforts made to promote a closer fellowship between brethren in different congregations. Past problems will be forgotten because love "taketh not account of evil."[6] Ethnic differences will be ignored because "you are all one in Christ Jesus."[7] Party loyalties will be erased because "neither the one who plants nor the one who waters is anything."[8]

Seventh, there will be an exposure of those who delight in and thrive on bringing division among brethren. They will be "marked."[9] They will be rejected after the first and second warning.[10]

Standards to Determine Fellowship

There is a threefold criterion by which one can determine who is included in the "in Christ" fellowship.

First, there is the criterion of identity. No one can be recognized as a brother in Christ who is not already a son of God. It does not make any difference how moral, pious or good an unbaptized believer might be. If he has not been born into the family of God in the new birth, he cannot be in fellowship with God's children.

Second, there is the criterion of doctrine. It does make a difference what one believes. He can believe a lie and be damned.[11] Those who seek to join the fellowship who do not bring the right teaching are to be tested[12] and rejected.[13] No one can be denied the right to believe anything he wants to believe, but he does not have the right to use the "in Christ" fellowship to deceive others.

Third is the criterion of practice. No matter how pious the claim that one makes of knowing Jesus, it must be regarded as a lie if he is not obeying His commandments.[14] Those whom Jesus does not know as His disciples are not to be regarded as brothers by those who do follow Him.

God has given man an absolute and objective way to judge who is "included in" and who must be "excluded from" fellowship in Christ.

Two things are involved. First, there is the absolute and objective revelation of God's will revealed in the Scriptures. Second, there are absolute and objective actions which can be observed in a person's life. By a comparison of these two things, one can discover who enjoys fellowship with God and hence may receive fellowship from the church. Alexander Campbell noted these two objective bases of making judgement in *The Christian System* .

Two things are paramount in all cases of discipline
being brought before a congregation — *the Fact and
the Law* . The fact is always to be established by good
testimony or by the confession of the transgressor.
The thing said to have been done, or the fact being
established, the next question is, *What is the law in
the case?* This the elders of the congregation must
decide. They are to be judges both of the fact and the
law. If they are not, they are unfit for the office and
unworthy of the name *"rulers"* of the congregation.[15]

Fellowship must not be extended on the basis of subjective judgment or
personal convenience. When such is done, fellowship is limited to only those
within one's own little circle. A fellowship based on such human ties might be
acceptable for a civic club or a social group, but such is not so in the church.

Jesus shows the folly of this kind of fellowship in the parable of the sheep
and goats. In the parable Jesus separates the goats from the sheep. The goats
were rejected because they refused to extend fellowship to Jesus' brothers who
were in need. Jesus' brothers were sick and hungry. Those who were called
goats left them unloved and unhelped. Jesus' brothers were strangers and in
prison. Those who were called goats were unconcerned and uncaring. Those
on the goat side tried to plead ignorance and said,

Lord, when did we see You hungry, or thirsty, or a stranger,
or naked, or sick, or in prison, and did not take care
of You?[16]

Jesus rejected their plea and pronouced a sobering judgment upon them
and all others who reject a Divinely decreed fellowship.

Truly I say to you, to the extent that you did not do it
to one of the least of these, you did not do it to Me.
And these will go away into eternal punishment...[17]

One cannot know the fellowship of Christ without participating in the
fellowship of His brethren. Neglecting to show fellowship by caring and
sharing with the least of Jesus' brothers will bring rejection at the
Judgment. One cannot know fellowship with Jesus without experiencing
fellowship with all of Jesus' brothers.

Fellowship must not be extended merely upon personal testimony. One can claim that which is not true. One can call Jesus "Lord" without really meaning it. One can pretend to be something he is not. One can have a mistaken understanding of what it means to "know Jesus." An experiential testimony of knowing Jesus or doing mighty works in His name is not a sufficient basis for extending fellowship in Christ.

Jesus clearly states this in His personal teachings. In the context of warning against false prophets who make great claims, but who produce bad fruits, Jesus said:

> Not every one who says to Me, "Lord, Lord," will enter
> the kingdom of heaven; but he who does the will of My
> Father, who is in heaven. Many will say to Me on that
> day, "Lord, Lord, did we not prophesy in Your name, and
> in Your name cast out demons, and in Your name perform
> many miracles?" And then I will declare to them, "I
> never knew you; DEPART FROM ME, YOU WHO PRACTICE
> LAWLESSNESS."[18]

It would appear that these false disciples were sincere. They no doubt thought they spoke the truth when they prophesied in the name of Jesus. They no doubt thought they were doing the Lord's work when they claimed to cast out demons and performed miracles in Jesus' name. They thought wrong!

They were either self deceived or hypocrites. Either way, they were responsible for their conduct. If their claims involved hypocrisy, then they were twice condemned.[19] They were dishonest as well as disobedient. If their claims were made in sincerity, they were self deceived. Such would not change the judgment of Jesus. Right practice — as well as personal sincerity — is essential for fellowship with Jesus.

Jesus did not know these false teachers even though they claimed to be His disciples and do miracles in His name. Obedience to the will of God is the criterion for being known by Jesus. If one is not obedient, then all kinds of miraculous claims will not bring him into fellowship with Christ. If one is not obedient, then the most conscientious sincerity will not bring one into fellowship with Christ. One can believe a lie and be damned.[20] One can be sincere and still be lost.

Fellowship should not be extended superficially or without investigation. John warns Christians about doing such.

> Beloved, do not believe every spirit, but test the spirits
> to see whether they are from God; because many false
> prophets have gone out into the world.[21]

Fellowship must not be extended on the basis of human standards. Human creeds, human traditions and human parties cannot be the bases of fellowship in Christ.

Such human standards of fellowship do two things. First, they reject the Divine standard of fellowship by substituting human standards. Second, they bring further division. All human standards, be they creeds, traditions or religious heirarchy — promote division. They contradict one another and change with time. The basis of fellowship in Christ is not so fragile.

Thomas Campbell in the *Declaration and Address* shows the folly of human standards as a basis of unity:

> But this we do sincerely declare, that there is nothing
> we have hitherto received as matter of faith or practice,
> which is not expressly taught and enjoined in the word
> of God, either in express terms, or approved precedent,
> that we would not heartily relinquish, that so we might
> return to the original constitutional unity of the
> Christian church.[22]

Fellowship in Christ must not be extended to those whose faith and practice is without scriptural authority. If the fruit of a person's life does not fit the revealed will of God, then he cannot claim the fellowship of Christ.

The restoration principle of "speak where the Bible speaks and be silent where the Bible is silent" is an attempt to call men back to the Divine standard of fellowship.

Fellowship in Christ has never been broken by anything the Bible teaches. It has always been broken by that which has been taught and practiced by the authority of men. If one's religious fellowship is based upon anything except that for which there is a "thus saith the Lord," then beware! Such a fellowship is from man, not God.

Fellowship in Christ is far too precious to be broken by self-willed men who demand in the name of "relevance" and "liberty" that which has no biblical basis. Such does not promote fellowship. It rather destroys it.

Those who refuse to bring that for which there is no scriptural authority into the faith and practice of the church are not destroying fellowship in Christ. They are rather preserving and defending the Divine standard of fellowship.

The only kind of "unity meeting" that can be valid is one for the purpose of Bible study. It makes little difference what men desire or what culture demands. It is of little consequence what present or past leaders say or have said. No confidence can be placed in the preference of most of the people most of the time in most places. In seeking religious unity one question must be at the center: "What does the Bible say?" Men cannot establish a valid criterion upon which fellowship in Christ may be obtained. They can only compare the fruit of a man's life with the revealed will of God. This alone can be the criterion of fellowship in Christ.

Valid Barriers to Fellowship

Every person who has experienced the new birth at baptism is a child of God. As a child of God he is a brother to every other child of God. As long as he sustains his fellowship with God, the church is to extend fellowship to him. If he breaks his fellowship with God through sin, deliberate error or indifference, then the church is to break fellowship with him. The church does not set the criteria for fellowship. It can only use the criteria that God has set in determining the scope and limits of fellowship.

There are two kinds of fellowship barriers which exist in the church. They must not be confused with one another. One is from God and the other is from man.

One kind of fellowship barrier is immovable. It has been set by God and must not be ignored. God has established limits of fellowship beyond which a Christian must not go.

God established impenitent sin in a person's life as a barrier to fellowship. The Corinthian church was rebuked for extending fellowship to an immoral brother.[23]

God established error taught by a false teacher as a barrier to fellowship. John instructs Christians to deny fellowship to teachers who refuse to abide in the doctrine of Christ.[24]

One must not change or compromise what God has decreed. When God disinherits a son, the church must acknowledge it. Ignoring or neglecting to acknowledge that a brother has broken fellowship with God is a twofold sin. First, it is rebellion against the Lordship of Jesus because of a refusal to uphold His authority. Second, it is a failure of brotherly love because of the unwillingness to correct a brother in sin.

Attitude Barriers to Fellowship

The immovable barriers to fellowship established by God cannot be broken. They must be maintained at all cost.

Other barriers to fellowship are of a different kind. They are attitude barriers established by men. It is these barriers which often cause broken fellowship within a congregation and within the brotherhood. They have no basis in the Scriptures, but they are raised by Christians who have cold and selfish hearts.

Hatred and animosity toward the church is a great barrier to fellowship. For motivation known only to God, some members like to berate the brotherhood. They do not like the church but cannot bring themselves to leave her. They become a people going where they don't want to go, doing things they don't want to do, with people they don't like, to please a God they don't love. They are themselves unhappy and seek to bring everybody else into their fellowship of misery.

A mentality among some, who at one time took delight in running down the denominations, seems now to vent their frustrations with vicious tongues and pens against the church. Immature church leaders, disgruntled preachers and disciplined members delight in repeating — and usually exaggerating — any weakness found in a congregation or the brotherhood. They seek to remain above the church as judges instead of helping brethren who are struggling to overcome their weakness.

It is odd that those who talk the most about how bad, narrow and bigoted the church is, are the very ones who do not want to use corrective discipline to make it better. They prefer to curse the darkness of error rather than light the candle of truth to make things better.

The "bad guys" are not the ones who teach the truth about disciplining false teachers but are the ones who teach error. The "bad guys" are not the ones who expose immorality but are the ones who practice it. The "bad guys" are not the ones who stay in the fellowship and try to make it better. They are the ones who leave the fellowship and try to justify their actions by running down the church.

An editorial by Howard Norton in the Christian Chronicle reproves this attitude.

Bad mouthing the church of Jesus Christ seems to
be a favorite pastime these days for some of our
erstwhile spiritual leaders. Although the cynics gladly

deposit their salary checks received from the people
they caricature and criticize, they reserve most of
their praise for churches, speakers and writers from
outside our fellowship. Like those who are too good to
enjoy being bad and too bad to enjoy being good, these
critics among us are too financially and emotionally
dependent on the church of Christ to leave it, but they
apparently resent it too much to see anything but its
warts and moles.

It is time for us to make evil-speaking about the church
an unacceptable behavior among God's people. Even
when there is a legitimate need to reprove and rebuke,
common sense tells us that there must be also words of
hope and praise for the church. It is time for spokesmen
to quit talking about the church as if it were God's enemy
and recognize that it is Christ's bride — purchased with
his own blood. It is time for us to speak good words
about the Lord's church.

Unless a church leader can sing, "I love thy church, O God,"
and mean it, he should hold his negative comments, resign
his position and get a secular job where he can make an
honest living.[25]

When men speak of the church of Christ as nothing more than a human
denomination, a historical movement or a socio-economic institution, they
reveal more about themselves and their own impoverished faith than they do
about the church.

The church has problems. It always has and always will. One does not
read of Paul criticizing the church in his letters. Certainly the church had
problems then. They were not ignored. He marked the false teachers, reproved
those who were divisive and even cast to Satan those who were the impenitent
and immoral.

He always maintained the ideal of the church in spite of the human
weaknesses of men. The church was the consumation of the eternal purpose of
God, the spotless bride of Christ and the holy dwelling place of the Holy Spirit.
Paul always spoke of the church in endearing terms — so do all of those who
love Jesus today.

Fear is one of the attitude barriers to fellowship. One is afraid to take the risk of rejection. He is afraid to expose himself to others when it might bring insult or injury. He is fearful of accepting others because he has been hurt by others in the past.

Such was the problem with the Jerusalem church when Saul sought their fellowship. He had been converted at Damascus but now sought to unite with the brethren at Jerusalem. One can understand their fear, since Saul had previously made havoc of the church in Jerusalem and cast Christians into prison because of their faith. Luke recorded the incident:

> And when he had come to Jerusalem, he was trying to
> associate with the disciples; and they were all afraid
> of him, not believing that he was a disciple.[26]

A Christian by the name of Barnabas rose above this fear and vouched for his conversion. He took the risk of fellowship and accepted a brother for who he was, not for who he had been.

There is a need today for more "influential brethren" like Barnabas to speak up for brothers who are under the cloud of unjust criticism. Denial of fellowship must not be practiced against those who have turned from their sin and error. Leaders of the church should not tolerate self-appointed ecclesiastical potentates who "blackball" innocent brethren. Fear of being "labeled" or "written up" must not stop one from affirming truth or supporting a worthy cause.

Ignorance is an attitude barrier to fellowship. It is easy to allow one's thinking to be hampered by pride and prejudice. The limited scope of one's associations, his uncritical reading and a willingness to believe biased reports sometimes cause one to be ignorant of the true situation. Without accurate understanding, he proceeds to draw lines of fellowship which God does not recognize.

It is just as wrong to deny fellowship to those who are in fellowship with God as it is to give fellowship to those whom God does not acknowledge.

Ignorance was involved when the Jewish brethren at Antioch denied fellowship to the Gentile Christians. They put up barriers which God had not given. This was done because of the influence of "certain men from James."[27] Reputable brethren like Peter and Barnabas were caught up in this schism. Luke records the incident:

> And some men came down from Judea and began
> teaching the brethren, "Unless you are circumcised
> according to the custom of Moses, you cannot be saved."[28]

These brethren were binding that which God had not bound. They were making a test of fellowship that which was without the authority of Christ. They had created a human barrier to fellowship.

The letter that was sent from the apostles at Jerusalem exposed the ignorance and corrected those who were ring leaders in disturbing the fellowship. Part of the letter reads as follows:

> "Since we have heard that some of our number to whom
> we gave no instruction have disturbed you with their
> words, unsettling your souls..."[29]

Binding that which God has not bound is wrong. Those who do so need to be corrected, for they disturb the fellowship and unsettle the souls of brethren. They cause unwarranted barriers to fellowship.

Selfishness is an attitude barrier to fellowship in Christ. Fellowship is denied because it might cost money, threaten one's power or injure his ego. Fellowship does cost. Many in the church at Jerusalem sold their possessions to take care of fellowship needs.[30] Fellowship does threaten power. Diotrephes refused fellowship to those sent by John because they were a threat to his power.[31] Fellowship can humble the ego. It demands on one hand the acceptance of those who are different and on the other hand the surrender of any faith or practice that is without Scriptural authority.

True fellowship is expensive. It costs to share with a brother who is in need. It costs to humble one's ego and surrender his own cherished desires and abide only by the Bible. Fellowship causes one to surrender his own rights to please others. Fellowship causes one to be a servant to all rather than exercise power over others. Paul teaches this aspect of fellowship.

> Let each of us please his neighbor for his good, to
> his edification. For even Christ did not please Himself...[32]

Perhaps the greatest barriers to fellowship are indifference and negligence. Fellowship is not strong when it is lightly regarded and loosely maintained. It is difficult to discover which precedes the other. Does poor fellowship breed indifference, or does indifference breed poor fellowship? Where one is found the other will soon be evident.

The book of Hebrews was written to discouraged, negligent Christians. It is clear that a major cause of their problems was the weakness of their fellowship. They neglected hospitality.[33] They neglected benevolence.[34] They were forsaking the Christian assemblies.[35] All of these things had to do with the fellowship of the church. Because of their neglected fellowship, they were discouraged. Since they were discouraged, they neglected fellowship.

The same thing happens in the twentieth century church. Christians grow weak because they neglect the demands and opportunities of fellowship. This neglect leads to a weaker fellowship which in turn leads to more negligence which in turn leads to an even weaker fellowship and so on. A Christian cannot survive without fellowship. He will die of discouragement.

Fear, ignorance, selfishness and indifference are all barriers to fellowship in Christ. These are set up by Satan to weaken and destroy the real fellowship known in Jesus Christ. They must be overcome if the church is to be healthy.

Fellowship Erases Barriers

Fellowship in Christ is greater than personal preferences or cultural conformity. It supercedes such barriers of alienation as racial differences, educational levels, cultural structures and economic advantages. Christianity is the great leveling plane. All who are in Christ are on the same level before God and in the church.

Historically, fellowship in Christ has been hindered because men have allowed other than Divine factors to determine fellowship. Identifying with a preacher party, lining up with a Gospel paper or following the thinking of a certain school has caused alienation of brothers who should have been one in Christ. Cultural differences, geographical separation and political sympathies have made brethren fearful of each other. This has contributed to a strain and sometimes a break in fellowship. This is wrong.

The death of Jesus on the cross broke down all such barriers between men.[36] This event was so great and full of unselfish love, that it completely obliterates all the different peculiarities that followers of Christ might have.

Endnotes

[1]See page 26.
[2]See page 27-28.

[3]Galatians 2:11-14.

[4]Matthew 5:23.

[5]I John 2:19.

[6]I Corinthians 13:5.

[7]Galatians 3:28.

[8]I Corinthians 3:7.

[9]Romans 16:17.

[10]Titus 3:10.

[11]II Thessalonians 2:11-12.

[12]I John 4:1.

[13]II John 11.

[14]I John 2:3-4.

[15]Alexander Campbell, *The Christian System* (Cincinnati: Standard Publishing Co., 1835), p. 68.

[16]Matthew 25:44.

[17]Matthew 25:45-46.

[18]Matthew 7:21-23.

[19]Luke 12:47-48. Jesus taught that one has greater responsibility when he knows the right but refuses to do it.

[20]II Thessalonian 2:11-12.

[21]I John 4:1.

[22]James DeForest Murch, *Christians Only* (Cincinnati: Standard Publishing, 1962), p. 44.

[23]I Corinthians 5:1-12.

[24]II John 9-11.

[25]Howard Norton, *Christian Chronicle* 45:6, "What's Right with the Church," (June 1988), p. 22.

[26]Acts 9:26.

[27]Galatians 2:12.

[28]Acts 15:1.

[29]Acts 15:24.

[30]Acts 2:44.

[31]III John 9.

[32]Romans 15:2-3.

[33]Hebrews 13:1-3.

[34]Hebrews 10:32-34.

[35]Hebrews 10:24-25.

[36]Ephesians 2:13-18.

Study Questions

1. Why is fellowship important?

2. Discuss the standards which determine fellowship.

3. Is one's attitude important in fellowship? How important?

4. Discuss the two kinds of valid barriers to fellowship.

5. How does fellowship erase barriers?

6/ The Breadth of Fellowship

> *"One can usually do more to correct error by teaching and admonishing than by debating and withdrawing."*
>
> *"This author has never known of one who has been disciplined for what he privately believes — but only for what he teaches and practices."*

A distinctive element of true Christianity is that it brings men together. Barriers which normally separate men into different parties are broken down. Ethnic characteristics which make men different are superceded by internal spiritual qualities which make men one. Diversity in backgrounds, interests and temperament — instead of being factors that divide, become strengths to aid the unity of the whole.

The breadth of the fellowship in Christ is a source of great power. There is strength in diversity — if that diversity is united in Christ. Just as each member of the physical body is different and yet contributes to the strength of the whole, each member of the church is different and yet contributes to the strength of the whole. If all members of the body of Christ were identical, there would be no body.

Peace Through the Cross

The cross is the means by which different kinds of people are brought together in the church. Nothing else could be strong enough to unite such different kinds of people.

> But now in Christ Jesus you who formerly were far off
> have been brought near by the blood of Christ. For He
> Himself is our peace, who made both groups into one, and
> broke down the barrier of the dividing wall, by abolishing
> in His flesh the enmity, which is the law of commandments
> contained in ordinances, that in Himself He might make the
> two into one new man, thus establishing peace, and might
> reconcile them both into one body to God through the cross.[1]

The cross not only erased the estrangement of man from God; it also broke down the wall which divided man from man. The very thing that made possible man's fellowship with God demands man's fellowship with all who are in God's family.

The Christian has blood ties with every other Christian in the world. The blood of Christ that cleansed his sins becomes the blood of the covenant to bind him to all of those who are in the blood-bought church.

This oneness is consumated at baptism. It is then that one becomes a part of the family of God, a member of Christ's body and the dwelling place of the Holy Spirit.[2]

False Notions of Fellowship

There were false notions even in the early church that sought to compromise the breadth of fellowship. Some tried to make fellowship narrower than God intended by excluding those who did not keep their traditions. Some tried to make fellowship narrower by developing a group above the common Christian.

The first group was much like the Jewish Pharisees. They wanted to add their own exclusive traditions to the teachings of Jesus. The Pharisees, who sought to "build a fence around the law,"[3] wanted to add circumcision as a requirement for salvation.[4] They excluded from their fellowship Gentiles who were not circumcised.[5] They sought to bind Jewish diet regulations and holy days upon the church.[6]

Paul was very zealous to refute such teachings. It was perhaps the most widespread false teaching that Paul confronted in the first century church. The teaching that focused on salvation by works of the law contradicted the very heart of the Gospel message — salvation by grace through faith. Such a teaching threatened the basis of fellowship in the church. People united in Christ were being divided because of the traditions of men. Paul was clear in refuting such teachings:

> See to it that no one takes you captive through
> philosophy and empty deception, according to the
> traditions of men, according to the elementary principles
> of the world, rather than according to Christ.[7]

> It was for freedom that Christ set us free; therefore
> keep standing firm and do not be subject again to a yoke
> of slavery. Behold I, Paul, say to you that if you receive
> circumcision, Christ will be of no benefit to you...
> You have been severed from Christ, you who are seeking
> to be justified by law; you have fallen from grace.[8]

Paul refused to let any brother—no matter how influential or noble his motive might be — to bind an unauthorized practice upon the church. Toleration of unauthorized human innovations would have divided the fellowship. It did at Antioch.[9] The "pro-circumcision" party demanded conformity to their human innovation. When others refused to conform, the church split.

The second group to threaten the fellowship of the early church is known mainly through the writings of John.[10] Some of this group's teachings conform to what later would be called Gnosticism. It would appear from the way they are refuted by John that they held to the following teachings:

They were above sin	I John 1:8-10
They did not keep commandments	I John 2:3-6
They had outgrown the fellowship	I John 2:19
They refused to do benevolence	I John 3:17-18
They did not believe Jesus was flesh	I John 4:2-3

They were saturated with Greek speculative philosophy that was dualistic. These false teachers seemed to believe that sins of the body did not involve the spirit — that physical benevolence was unrelated to spiritual values — that keeping the commandments or obeying the word was too much a part of the physical world for them to be concerned with. They were in the "know."[11] They believed they had secret knowledge intuitively received from God that was better than the word of God. They felt themselves to be "supersaints" above the regular Christians in the fellowship, so they went out from among the brethren.

This group threatened the fellowship of the church in the second century. It divided believers into two classes.

The higher class, according to their teaching, consisted of the *pneumatic* Christian who had received "secret knowledge." They were unconcerned with such lowly things as understanding the word, keeping commandments or giving physical benevolence. They were redeemed by *gnosis* .

The lower class, according to their teaching, were *psychic* Christians redeemed by faith. They were involved with physical things like commandments, ethics and benevolence. They had no "secret knowledge" and therefore were on a lower spiritual plane.

John was zealous to refute this false teaching. It was to become a major threat to the church. Using the vocabulary of the false teachers, John refutes the basic elements of their error:

If we say that we have no sin, we are deceiving ourselves, and the truth is not in us.[12]

And by this we know that we have come to know Him, if we keep His commandments. The one who says, "I have come to know Him," and does not keep His commandments, is a liar and the truth is not in him;[13]

They went out from us, but they were not really of us; for if they had been of us, they would have remained with us.[14]

But whoever has the world's goods, and beholds his brother in need and closes his heart against him, how does the love of God abide in him?[15]

By this you know the Spirit of God: every spirit that confesses that Jesus Christ has come in the flesh is from God.[16]

Those who left the fellowship of Christians because of this teaching felt spiritually superior. They possessed an experiential faith that they viewed as above evil matter. Their knowledge was above the word. Their actions were not governed by commandments. Their ethics were above the word. They looked down on the church and felt they had outgrown it.

Toleration of this error in the church would have destroyed the fellowship. John teaches that those who left the church were no longer to receive fellowship from the church. The very fact that they left showed that "they were not of us." It is folly to seek to extend fellowship to those who have left the church. The very nature of fellowship makes it an impossibility.

When someone leaves the church, it becomes impossible to withdraw fellowship from him. One cannot withdraw that which is not there. The very fact of his withdrawal from the church places him outside of the realm of effective discipline. If the fellowship of the church had meant anything to him, he would not have left it.

This does not mean the church should do nothing. Following the pattern established in I John, one is to recognize that such a brother has left the fellowship. This recognition would involve a change in relationship similar to that involved in church discipline. Fellowship has been broken and members of the church can no longer extend an "in Christ" fellowship to the brother who has left. The church does not "withdraw fellowship;" it only recognizes that fellowship has been broken.

The Scope of Fellowship

The scope of "in Christ" fellowship must be broad enough to include all types of people. Included in this fellowship are people with ethnic differences like Jews and Gentiles; people with social differences like master and slaves; people with gender differences like male and female.

There is neither Jew nor Greek, there is neither slave nor free man, there is neither male nor female; for you are all one in Christ Jesus.[17]

In the church at Corinth there were Christians like Erastus the city treasurer[18] and bond slaves.[19] There were Christians who had been brought up as Jews with high moral values and others whose pagan backgrounds had involved them in the very depth of immorality.[20] Some of the Corinthian Christians had

Koinonia

rich backgrounds in the law of Moses, while some had Greek philosophical roots. In Christ they were all one body. The power of the Gospel is demonstrated by the fact that such diversity could be united.

The "in Christ" fellowship has no room for exclusive cliques, ethnic separations or social divisions. Walls that separate men on these grounds have been broken down and cannot exist in the church.

As the different instruments of an orchestra are harmonized into one sound that supercedes the beauty of any one instrument, so is the fellowship of the church. The diversity of each individual member of the church is overcome by the united harmony found in full fellowship.

The scope of "in Christ" fellowship must be broad enough to include those of different opinions. This area of tension often causes the greatest strain in Christian fellowship.

It is difficult to distinguish opinion from faith. What one might regard as faith, another might regard as opinion. In a general way, one might define an opinion as that for which there is no "thus saith the Lord." If one is able to show that Scriptures teach something, it is no longer an opinion. It must be regarded as a matter of faith.

Paul makes a distinction between opinion (a personal judgment) and faith (based on a commandment from the Lord):

Now concerning virgins I have no command of the Lord,
but I give an opinion as one who by the mercy of the
Lord is trustworthy...[21]

Paul had an opinion about the wisdom of virgins marrying, but he did not bind this opinion on others.

There are three things about matters of opinion which one should understand in order to distinguish it from matters of faith.

First, an opinion is a private matter, not a public teaching. One's opinion must not be bound on others. In the context of a difference in judgment about the eating of meat at Rome, Paul shows one must respect the opinions of others:

Let not him who eats regard with contempt him who
does not eat, and let not him who does not eat judge him
who eats, for God has accepted him.[22]

Second, an opinion is binding on the person who holds it but not on others who do not. If one holds an opinion that a certain practice is wrong even though he cannot prove it from the Scriptures, then he should not do it. He refuses to do it—not because it can be shown to be wrong from the Scriptures—but because it is against his own conscience. Paul teaches this principle of conduct:

> The faith which you have, have as your own conviction
> before God. Happy is he who does not condemn himself
> in what he approves. But he who doubts is condemned
> if he eats, because his eating is not from faith.[23]

A Christian is more demanding of himself than others. To go against one's own opinion is to violate one's conscience. This is wrong, whether or not his opinion is correct. A Christian does not bind his opinion on others. That would be selfish egotism. One's own personal standards are more demanding on himself than on others.

Third, there should be an acceptance of those who hold to different opinions. The opinion issues of the first century centered around eating meats, special days and circumcision. Paul deals with the principles involved and shows how men with different opinions can live in harmony. The exhortations he gave to the Romans are just as relevant today, even though the issues may be different:

> Now we who are strong ought to bear the weaknesses
> of those without strength and not just please ourselves.
> Let each of us please his neighbor for his good, to his
> edification. For even Christ did not please Himself...
> Wherefore, accept one another, just as Christ also
> accepted us to the glory of God.[24]

The scope of "in Christ" fellowship must be broad enough to include those in all of the different stages of spiritual maturity. One must consider maturity levels when he judges the conduct of fellow Christians. It would be nice if all Christians were spiritually mature, unselfish and kind. This, however, is not the case. It was not the case in the first century and it is not the case now. There are still Christians who are egocentric like babies and rebellious like adolescents. They are not to be despised for their immaturity any more than one would despise children in a physical family for acting in a childish way.

Unacceptable behavior is not justified for either the mature or the immature. The different stages of an individual's maturity does help one to understand how best to respond to a situation. The response that one would give to a ten-month-old baby putting food in its hair is different from the response one would give to a ten-year-old child. The conduct might be the same, but the maturity level is different. In the same way one must consider the maturity level of a Christian when responding to his misconduct.

There were Christians at Corinth who were too immature to receive strong teachings.[25] Some were so self-centered in their use of spiritual gifts that they had to be admonished to "grow up" or be mature.[26] Immaturity was a factor in the party spirit which was dividing them. Immaturity was a factor in their abuse of the Lord's Supper, immodest dress and even doubting the resurrection. They were still in fellowship despite their immaturity.

There is much immaturity in the church today. It is the cause of much tension and the root of many problems. Childish selfishness is reflected in those who make a fuss when things do not go their way. Adolescent rebellion is reflected in those who brashly demand their rights without consideration for the feelings of others.

Such conduct is exasperating. One is tempted to withdraw fellowship from those who act so immature. Not so! They are an important part of the body. The church is to "grow them up," not "cut them off." Paul affirms the importance of even the weakest member of the body:

...On the contrary, it is much truer that the members
of the body which seem to be weaker are necessary.[27]

Immature babies and growing adolescents are important in the family. They are cherished in love. They are not kicked out of the family because of their childishness. The family helps them to mature by giving them support and discipline. The same kind of supportive love is demanded in the family of God.

Immaturity should not be accepted without correction. "Young" church babies, without correction, will grow up to be "old" church babies. They are not being helped by ignoring their immaturity. The writer of Hebrews shamed those who refused to grow up.

For though by this time you ought to be teachers,
you have need again for some one to teach you the
elementary principles of the oracles of God, and you
have come to need milk and not solid food. [28]

Childish actions may be cute when seen in a child trying to mature. Childish actions are obnoxious, however, when seen in a grown man who is still acting like a baby.

The "in Christ" fellowship must be broad enough to involve those with doctrinal misunderstandings. This does not mean that doctrine is unimportant or that the practice of error is to be tolerated in the church. When a brother has a doctrinal misunderstanding, one can and must do a lot of things before excluding him from the fellowship. The first response to a brother who holds to a doctrinal error is teaching. Priscilla and Aquila took Apollos aside and taught him the way of the Lord more accurately.[29] One can usually do more to correct error by teaching and admonishing than by debating and withdrawing.

Paul could tolerate those at Corinth who questioned the resurrection. He did not ignore the error, but reasoned with them in order to bring them to a correct understanding.[30] A large part of the Christians with Jewish backgrounds in the first century continued to believe that the observance of the law of Moses was essential to salvation. Such misunderstanding was tolerated until they began to bind it on others.[31]

There is a difference in a doctrinal misunderstanding and teaching a false doctrine.

Paul tolerated those at Corinth who had doubts about the resurrection and addressed them as "saints." He did not ignore their error, but sought to teach them the truth on the matter in I Corinthians 15.

The situation was different at Ephesus. Here Hymenaeus was teaching a false doctrine that the resurrection had already taken place. Such could not be tolerated.

> ...keeping faith and a good conscience, which some
> have rejected and suffered shipwreck in regard to their
> faith. Among these are Hymenaeus and Alexander, whom
> I have delivered over to Satan...[32]

> But avoid worldly and empty chatter, for it will lead to
> further ungodliness, and their talk will spread like
> gangrene. Among them are Hymenaeus and Philetus, men
> who have gone astray from the truth saying that the
> resurrection has already taken place, and thus they upset
> the faith of some.[33]

There is a difference in doctrinal misunderstanding and teaching a false doctrine. At Corinth, Paul tolerated those who questioned the resurrection and sought to teach them the way of the Lord more perfectly. Such was not possible at Ephesus. Hymenaeus and others were teaching a faith-destroying doctrine. They had to be disciplined.

One sometimes meets a brother who has been disciplined by the church who tries to justify himself by claiming "doctrinal liberty." He thought his discipline was because of his "private belief" in some questionable doctrine. He whines over the severity of the brethren. Upon investigation it is found that what he considered a "private belief" was in reality a false doctrine which he taught to create a schism. What he considered a private incident — that would not bother anyone else — was in reality a public practice affecting the faith of others. This author has never known of one who has been disciplined for what he privately believes — but only for what he teaches and practices.

In discussing the division within the Restoration Movement at the turn of the twentieth century, Winfred Garrison makes a similar observation:

> The specific question was whether or not the absence
> of instrumental music in the apostolic churches implied
> a permanent divine command not to have it. Here was a
> matter in which belief would naturally lead to action.
> The anti-organ party never withdrew from a church
> because a majority of its members *believed* that it
> would be proper to have an organ. They withdrew only
> when an organ was put in. Disciples have never had
> really serious controversy over beliefs; their conflicts
> have always been about courses of action.[34]

Christians in the early church had different understandings of the resurrection. Some of these views were erroneous. These different understandings did not break fellowship until they were taught and began to destroy the faith of others.[35] Christians in the early church had different understandings about circumcision. Some of these views were erroneous. These different understandings did not break the fellowship until the actions of the Jews caused fellowship to be broken.[36]

Fellowship in Christ is broad. It can include all types of people, all kinds of opinions, all stages of spiritual maturity and even doctrinal misunderstandings. Toleration of diversity, acceptance of weaknesses and unselfish love of the brethren are musts for an "in Christ" fellowship.

Chart #4 The scope of fellowship in Christ must be broad enough to include all kinds of people who have been born into God's family. Though their temperaments are different, they are one in the spirit. Though their maturity levels are different, they are all a part of the family. Though their opinions are different, they are united together in faith. Though doctrine might not be clearly understood by everyone in the same way, they are open to correction and growth.

Scope of Fellowship

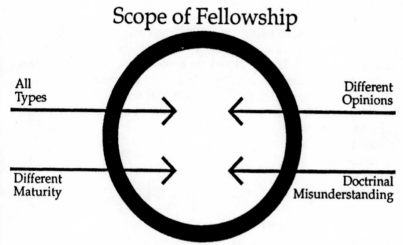

All Types → ← Different Opinions

Different Maturity → ← Doctrinal Misunderstanding

"...there is no distinction between Greek and Jew, circumcised and uncircumcised, barbarian, Scythian, slave and freeman, but Christ is all, and in all."
— Colossians 3:11

Endnotes

[1]Ephesians 2:13-16.
[2]Galatians 3:26-28; I Corinthians 12:13.
[3]This concept arose from a statement in the Mishnah which had been handed down in Rabbinic traditions. The statement said, "Moses received theTorah from Sinai and delivered it to Joshua, and Joshua to the elders, and the elders to the prophets, and the prophets delivered it to the men of the Great Synagogue. They said three things: Be deliberate in judgment, raise up many disciples, and make a fence for the Torah". The "fence around the law" consisted of the traditions handed down by the Rabbi.

These traditions were there to keep a man from even coming close to breaking the law. See E. C. Blackman, *Biblical Interpretation,* London: The Westminster Press, 1957, p. 66.

[4]Acts 15:1.

[5]Galatians 2:12.

[6]Colossians 2:16-17.

[7]Colossians 2:8.

[8]Galatians 5:1-2, 4.

[9]Galatians 2:12.

[10]In refuting this group John showed six things basic to fellowship: (1) Walking in the light, I John 1:6-7; (2) The blood of Jesus, 1:7; (3) Keeping the commandments, 2:3; (4) Loving the brethren, 2:10; 4:16; (5) Confessing Jesus came in the flesh, 2:23; 5:10-12; (6) Not continuing in sin, 3:6-10.

[11]*Gnosis* words are used 41 times in the five chapters of I John. It is translated "know" and is the term which was later to be used to identify the sect known as "Gnostics."

[12]I John 1:8.

[13]I John 2:3-4.

[14]I John 2:19.

[15]I John 3:17.

[16]I John 4:2.

[17]Galatians 3:28. See also I Corinthians 12:13.

[18]Romans 16:23.

[19]I Corinthians 7:21-24.

[20]I Corinthians 10:1-4; 6:9-11.

[21]I Corinthians 7:25.

[22]Romans 14:3.

[23]Romans 14:22-23.

[24]Romans 15:1-3, 7.

[25]I Corinthians 3:1-2.

[26]I Corinthians 14:20.

[27]I Corinthians 12:22.

[28]Hebrews 5:12.

[29]Acts 18:26.

[30]I Corinthains 15:1-58.

[31]Acts 15:1-29.

[32]I Timothy 1:19-20.

[33]II Timothy 2:16-18.

[34]Winfred E. Garrison, *Christian Unity and Disciples of Christ* (St. Louis: The

Bethany Press, 1955), p. 214.
[35]I Timothy 1:20; II Timothy 2:17-18.
[36]Galatians 2:12.

Study Questions

1. Discuss barriers often found in practicing Christian fellowship.

2. What are some of the false ideas people have about fellowship? In what ways can these ideas be corrected?

3. In practicing fellowship, where does the idea of one's personal opinion fit in? How can we allow for personal opinion in which two brothers may differ and still maintain fellowship?

4. Discuss how different levels of maturity affect fellowship.

5. How does "in Christ" fellowship deal with doctrinal misunderstandings? Does this mean that doctrine is not important?

7 / The Limits of Fellowship

"One does not choose his brother. He can only recognize him as a brother when God recognizes him as a son."

"One cannot expect to be in heaven with those to whom he has refused fellowship on the earth."

"God does not have 'step children' or 'sons-in-law' in His family."

The basis of Christian fellowship does not rest with inherited genes, academic ability, ethnic origins or economic status. Most groupings of men are based on such ties. Not so with the church. The basis of Christian fellowship is found in Divinity. Those in fellowship with one another as brothers in the church know this relationship only because they are in fellowship with God as their Father.

One does not choose his brother. He can only recognize him as a brother when God recognizes him as a son. Human differences are irrelevant. If a person is God's child, Jesus' disciple, and a possessor of the Holy Spirit, he is in full fellowship with the church. He is a recipient of all the rights and privileges of God's family.

A man's wife dies and leaves him several children. He holds the family together with great difficulty for a period of time. He later meets a lady whom he learns to love. They are married. The lady accepts more than just her husband when she becomes his wife. She accepts his children and becomes their step-mother. She becomes a wife and mother at the same time. All of the children come with the marriage.

A similar situation exists when one becomes a Christian. When he is born into God's family, he becomes a child of God. At the same time he becomes a brother to all of God's other children. The same thing that made him a son also made him a brother. All of God's children come with the bargain.

One must be zealous not to withhold fellowship from those who are in God's family. One cannot expect to be in heaven with those to whom he has refused fellowship on the earth.

One must be just as zealous to deny fellowship to those who are out of God's fellowship. If God does not recognize a person as His son, one must not recognize him as a brother. If God has removed one of His sons from the fellowship of the family circle, such must be recognized by the rest of God's family. A Christian must not give to another a fellowship that has been denied by God.

One must not be indifferent about fellowship in the church. It is wrapped up in one's own relationship with God.

To open fellowship to those whom God does not recognize is to humanize the church and usurp the authority of God. Such does not help in overcoming the estrangement they have with God. It only reflects a disregard for God's authority and extends false hope to the estranged.

To deny fellowship to those God accepts is also to humanize the church and usurp the authority of God. Binding what God has not bound in the name of tradition or personal preference does not change the will of God. It only reflects the ignorance and hard hearts of the ecclesiastical enforcers.

Fellowship is determined by Divinity. Woe be to any man who usurps this prerogative .... be it to bind that which is not bound or loose that which is not loosed.

Brotherhood is broader than fellowship. Not all of God's children are in fellowship with the church.

Some of God's children are disinherited sons. God has cut them off from His family. They departed from the faith. They fell from grace. They returned to the world. They are still sons of God — they cannot be unborn — but they are no longer in fellowship with him. They have been disinherited. They are lost. The blood of Christ no longer cleanses their sins since they no longer "walk in the light."[1]

The axiom is true that states, "nothing should be made a test of fellowship which is not a condition of salvation." Fellowship is to be withdrawn from a brother in the church only when his conduct places him in a lost condition. If such a one has fallen from God's grace, then he should not be in fellowship with God's children.

Some of God's children are prodigal sons. They have left the Father's house and no longer desire His fellowship. God did not cut them off. They left of their own free will.[2] Like the father of the prodigal son, God desires for them to return. He would joyfully receive them back into fellowship if they would repent and return. God does not force His fellowship on His children who desire to live in a far land or who are content to remain in a pig pen. When one's relationship with God is that of a prodigal son, the church must recognize him as a wayward brother.

There is a difference between fellowship and brotherhood. All who are in fellowship are brothers, but not all brothers are in fellowship.[3]

Christianity is exclusive as well as inclusive. Not all whom God desires to be saved will be saved.[4] Not all who call Jesus "Lord" are His disciples.[5] Not all who attend the Christian assemblies are in fellowship with God. There is more to Christian fellowship than sitting on the same pew or having one's name on the roll.

There are some very definite groups who are out of fellowship with God and should be out of fellowship with His church. The family of God is not to extend fellowship to those who have been rejected by the Father. If the fellowship of the church is broader than God's family, then it ceases to be His church. The church of Christ is exclusive. It excludes all of those who are not in fellowship with God.

Non-Children

The church cannot include in its fellowship those who are not children of God. There is no basis of fellowship for such individuals. They are not children of God; therefore, they cannot be brothers in God's family. They have not experienced the "new birth" or received the Holy Spirit.[6]

God does not have "step children" or "sons-in-law" in His family. It is true that non-Christians are often emotionally drawn to the fellowship of the church because of personal relationships with Christian friends or family. They might attend the assemblies, give contributions and engage in social activities with the church. Such can be a powerful influence to cause them to want to become Christians—to be born into the family. They cannot, however, know an "in Christ" fellowship until they become Christians. Fellowship in

Christ can only be known to those who are His genuine disciples.

The fact that a person is religious and believes in Jesus does not make him a child of God or a brother in the church. Some believers are rejected by Jesus because they are not obedient to His teachings.[7] If such are rejected by Jesus, they should not be received by His church.

Pretending a person is a Christian and in fellowship with God does not make it so. It is deceitful to do so under the guise of tolerance. It may please people in a social context, but it is dishonest. It gives a false sense of hope to the lost and destroys all motivation for evangelism.

Excluded from fellowship in God's family are all of those who have not been baptized into Christ.

Prodigal Sons

The church cannot retain in its fellowship those who have left it. Many, like the prodigal son, have left the Father's house on their own volition. The prodigal son was still a part of the family, but he could not have fellowship in the father's house until he returned from his wanderings. The father did not go to the pigpen to have fellowship with his rebellious son — he only waited for his return.

Many Christians have left the church. The truthfulness of this is demonstrated in many congregations by comparing the "membership directory" with those who regularly meet in the assemblies. Being on the "membership roll" does not mean that such a one is in fellowship with God.

People leave the fellowship of God's family for many reasons. Some espouse another faith. Some leave because of neglect and indifference. Some leave because of moral problems or materialistic concerns. Whatever their reason for leaving, one thing is sure, Christ will not ignore it.

Every branch in Me that does not bear fruit, He takes away; and every branch that bears fruit, He prunes it, that it may bear more fruit... Abide in Me, and I in you. As the branch cannot bear fruit of itself, unless it abides in the vine, so neither can you, unless you abide in Me... for apart from Me you can do nothing. If anyone does not abide in Me, he is thrown away as a branch, and dries up; and they gather them, and cast them into the fire, and they are burned.[8]

One cannot stay in fellowship with God and be unfruitful. God cuts such branches off. The church should also recognize what God has done with those "unfruitful" branches. If God cast them into the fire, it seems doubtful that the church should keep them on the roll.

Fellowship in the church is for those who remain in fellowship with God. One does not take a "leave of absence" from either God or the church.

When a brother leaves the church, this action brings out into the open what was already in his heart. He had ceased to be a real part of the fellowship — so he left it. He was already "out of fellowship" with God, or he would not have wanted to be "out of fellowship" with His children.

The Scriptures teach how the church is to respond to those who leave the church by their own choice:

> They went out from us, but they were not really of us;
> for if they had been of us, they would have remained
> with us; but they went out, in order that it might be
> shown that they all are not of us. [9]

These Christians had left the fellowship by choice. The church did not withdraw fellowship from them. They withdrew fellowship from the church. Discipline was not involved. Those who left felt no fellowship with the church. It would be difficult to withdraw that which does not exist. The church only acknowledged what had already taken place.

Disobedient Children

The church cannot retain in its fellowship those who do not follow apostolic teachings. Paul dealt with such a problem in the church at Thessalonica. Some Christians there were living unruly lives in disobedience to apostolic traditions. The rest of the church was told, "keep aloof" from them and "do not associate" with them.

> Now we command you, brethren, in the name of our
> Lord Jesus Christ, that you keep aloof from every brother
> who leads an unruly life and not according to the
> tradition which you received from us... And if anyone
> does not obey our instruction in this letter, take special
> note of that man and do not associate with him, so that
> he may be put to shame.[10]

The cause for breaking fellowship was that some of the brothers were sponging off of the church and refusing to work.[11] Why they were doing this is uncertain. They might have been expecting the immediate return of Jesus and had quit working to wait for the *parousia* . Certainly there was some misunderstanding in the church in Thessalonica about the coming of the Lord.[12] They might have been just plain lazy and were abusing Christian hospitality by mooching off of the brethren. Either way, the solution to the problem was the same.

> If anyone will not work, neither let him eat.[13]

The cause for limiting the fellowship to such brothers was their disobedience. They were not living "according to the tradition"[14] which had been given by an apostle. They were not following Paul's example and were refusing his order.[15] They were refusing to follow the instructions they had received verbally and in a letter.[16]

Disobedience to apostolic tradition and/or disobedience to apostolic instructions demanded discipline from the church. Such individuals were excluded from the fellowship.

It should be noted that it was the traditions from the *apostles*, not the traditions from *men*, that were to be followed.[17] Jesus condemned those who used the traditions of men as a standard of religious conduct.

> And why do you yourselves transgress the commandment
> of God for the sake of your tradition? ...And thus you
> invalidated the word of God for the sake of your
> tradition.[18]

The church must not retain in its fellowship those who refuse to obey apostolic traditions, apostolic instructions or apostolic orders as revealed in the Scriptures. Paul placed the denial of fellowship to such persons above the realm of human judgment and personal preference. He commanded it "in the name of our Lord Jesus Christ."[19] Those who disobey were still brothers and not to be regarded as enemies. Denying fellowship to them was an act of love, not of hateful retaliation. The purpose of "keeping aloof" from them and "not associating" with them was to shame them into repentance.

Children of God who love their Father will seek to keep other children of God from being disobedient to the Father's will. Brotherhood can best be expressed by mutual love, respect and obedience to the common Father.

False Teachers

The church cannot retain in its fellowship those who are false teachers. They become a leaven to destroy the faith of others.[20] Their false teachings cause God to break fellowship with them.[21] They fall under the anathema of God.[22] They cause division in the church by leading a party.[23]

It is not a sign of love to tolerate false teachers in the fellowship of the church. It is a sign of a "lack of love" toward those who are led astray by their false doctrine. It is a sign of a "lack of love" toward the false teacher when his error is not refuted. Using truth to refute error is not the act of a hateful enemy, but the conduct of a loving friend.[24]

The bond of Christian fellowship is one of the most powerful weapons there is to recall a brother from his error. If one really loves the church and has strong fellowship ties in it, he will do some deep soul searching before he allows himself to be carried away into speculative philosophy. If it becomes necessary for him to be disciplined by these brothers whom he loves, it will cause him to do some prayerful soul searching and serious restudy of what he is teaching. Paul recommended such a brotherly admonition be given to some unruly Christians in Thessalonica:

> And yet do not regard him as an enemy, but admonish
> him as a brother.[25]

Paul recognized that where fellowship was strong, it would be hard for false teachers to find a foothold. Where fellowship is weak, it would be hard to keep the weak from being overcome by error. When discipline is not practiced in the church, error is able to have free course.

It has been suggested that the only doctrine which can be made a "test of fellowship" is one's denial of Jesus Christ coming in the flesh. Winfred E. Garrison, followed by a multitude of other authors, took such a view:

> What I am really saying is that all those who regard
> Jesus as Lord are actually members of his Church and
> are within one brotherhood and fellowship, and that
> all other arrangements and relationships among
> individuals and groups are secondary to this dominating
> truth and should be designed in the light of a vivid
> realization of it.[26]

It is true that this error was part of what was being taught by the false teachers of II John 9-11.[27] A careful examination of the total context would indicate that the teachings of these false teachers involved more. They not only denied the humanity of Jesus, but were not walking "according to His commandments."[28]

If John were teaching that the only criterion for fellowship is confessing that Jesus came in the flesh, some serious theological problems would follow. If such an understanding is correct, then one must have fellowship with demons. They are believers in Jesus Christ.[29] If such an understanding is correct, then one has fellowship with those whom Jesus does not know. The non-doers of God's will are not recognized by Jesus as being His disciples.[30] If such an understanding is correct, then one must have fellowship with those God does not know. Those who claim to know Him but refuse to keep His commandments are liars. No matter how emotional their claim, refusal to keep His commandments and His word alienates one from God.[31]

Condoning false teachers in the church is not a sign of tolerance and love. It is a sign of the compromising fear of men and a blatant disrespect for the authority of Christ.

Schismatics

The church cannot retain in its fellowship those who are schismatics. Those who cause division among brethren are not to be allowed to go unchecked in the church. Paul taught such to the divided church at Corinth.[32] The elders at Ephesus were warned against allowing false church leaders to draw away disciples after their own party.[33]

Church parties are one of the greatest barriers to fellowship in the church. Those who cause them are to be "marked"[34] and "rejected."

> Now I urge you, brethren, keep your eye on those who
> cause dissensions and hindrances contrary to the
> teaching which you learned, and turn away from them.
> For such men are slaves, not of our Lord Christ but of
> their own appetites; and by their smooth and flattering
> speech they deceive the hearts of the unsuspecting.[35]

> Reject a factious man after a first and second warning,
> knowing that such a man is perverted and is sinning,
> being self-condemned.[36]

These passages tell several things about schismatics in the church. First, their motives are selfish. Second, they use deceitful means to influence the unsuspecting. Third, their teaching is contrary to apostolic teaching. Fourth, they create dissensions and factions. Fifth, they are to be "watched," "turned away from" and "rejected."

Jude described the schismatics of his day and warned the church about what they will do to the fellowship of the church:

> These men are those who are hidden reefs in your love
> feasts when they feast with you without fear, caring for
> themselves; clouds without water, carried along by winds;
> autumn trees without fruit, doubly dead, uprooted; wild
> waves of the sea, casting up their own shame like foam;
> wandering stars, for whom the black darkness has been
> reserved forever... These are grumblers, finding fault,
> following after their own lusts; they speak arrogantly,
> flattering people for the sake of gaining an advantage...
> These are the ones who cause divisions, worldly-minded,
> devoid of the Spirit.[37]

These schismatics were selfish, proud and fault-finders. They, like hidden reefs in the sea which destroy ships, are instruments of destruction in the fellowship of the church. They cause division and will ultimately be judged.[38]

Schismatics will be judged by God for their destructive behavior in the fellowship of the church. They also must be judged by the church itself. Those who cause division in the church must not be tolerated. The body of Christ must cut off any member who is divisive. If they do not, the body itself will be destroyed. Every church split could have been prevented if the church had excluded the schismatics from its fellowship before they formed a party.

The Immoral

The church cannot retain in its fellowship those who practice immorality. The reason is basic. The church is the holy temple of God — the dwelling place of the Holy Spirit.[39] Immorality in the church desecrates its holiness.

Paul affirms the holiness of the church as a basis for not making compromising alliances with unbelievers.[40] He compares the holy church to the holy temple of the Old Testament and shows how that holiness demanded those in the church to be separate from the defilement of flesh.

99

Koinonia

For we are the temple of the living God; just as God
said, "I WILL DWELL IN THEM AND WALK AMONG THEM;
AND I WILL BE THEIR GOD, AND THEY SHALL BE MY PEOPLE.
Therefore, COME OUT FROM THEIR MIDST AND BE SEPARATE,"
says the Lord. "AND DO NOT TOUCH WHAT IS UNCLEAN;"
...Therefore, having these promises, beloved, let us cleanse
ourselves from all defilement of flesh and spirit, perfecting holiness in
the fear of God.[41]

The theological basis of rejecting immorality in the church is the holiness of
God's people. Immorality desecrates the Christian's body in whom the Holy
Spirit dwells.[42] Immorality desecrates the church that is described as the
temple of God.

Those who practice immorality cut themselves off from God. It is the
responsibility of the church to recognize this in a practical way. Immorality has
no place in the fellowship of the saints.[43] Such was the clear apostolic instructions to the church at Ephesus.

But do not let immorality or any impurity or greed
even be named among you, as is proper among saints;
...For this you know with certainty, that no immoral
or impure person or covetous man, who is an idolater,
has an inheritance in the kingdom of Christ and God...
Therefore do not be partakers with them;... And do
not participate in the unfruitful deeds of darkness, but
instead even expose them.[44]

It is clear that the apostle wanted those who practiced immorality excluded
from the fellowship of the church. Immorality is totally incompatible with the
holiness of saints. Those who practice such will not inherit the kingdom of God
and should not "be partakers" with those in the kingdom of God, the church.

The church at Corinth was reproved for tolerating immoral Christians in
their fellowship. Instead of being ashamed of such conduct in their fellowship,
they were boasting about it with arrogance. The text does not reveal the content
of their boast. Was it that they gloried in a "cheap grace" without repentance?
Was it that they gloried in the open-minded tolerance and let every man do
what was right in his own eyes? Was it that they gloried in having a "liberal
spirit" and refused to be shackled with ethical rules or moral commandments?
The text does not say. Any of the above possibilities have been put forth a

100

multitude of times since the beginning of the church. The text is clear in instructing what was to be done in the situation.

> In the name of our Lord Jesus, when you are assembled,
> and I with you in spirit, with the power of our Lord Jesus,
> I have decided to deliver such a one to Satan... I wrote
> to you not to associate with any so-called brother if he
> should be an immoral person, or covetous, or an idolater,
> or a reviler, or a drunkard, or a swindler — not even to
> eat with such a one... Remove the wicked man from
> among yourselves.[45]

The basic reason Paul gives for such drastic action is threefold. First, such was necessary to recall the brother from his immorality. They were to care enough for his soul to correct that which would damn it.[46] Second, such was necessary to maintain the holiness of the church. Just as Jews were to take all leaven from their houses for the feast of unleaven bread, Christians were to take the defiling sin of immorality out of the church.[47] Third, such was necessary because toleration of immorality influences others to be immoral. A little leaven penetrates a whole loaf of bread and a little unchecked immorality will bring corruption to a whole church.[48]

One, no doubt, could make up an emotional story to support the immoral brother at Corinth and gain sympathy from many in the church. Consider these hypothetical circumstances.

Perhaps the brother who became immoral had been away from Corinth for many years. In the meanwhile, his mother had died and his father had married a much younger woman. It was not a very compatible marriage. May and December are far removed from one another in every way. The wife was frustrated being married to an older man.

When the son returned home, things began to sparkle around the house again. The son and the wife were near the same age. They were attracted to one another. Friendship turned to passion. The son took his father's wife for himself.

There was a lot of talk in the church since they were all supposed to be Christians. Perhaps the talk would sound something like this:

> Have you heard the latest about our young sister? You
> know, the one who is married to that old man. Well,
> her stepson has returned home and — would you

believe — they have fallen in love. She left that old
man and is now living with his son. They seem so happy.

Oh, I know that it is not right. But they make such a
nice-looking couple. They seem to be so much in love —
all the world loves a lover — How can anything so right
be wrong?

I don't know if they are going to church or not. You know
some of the brethren might take a dim view of all of this.
Give them a little time. If they will just not force the
issue and still come to church, it won't be long before they
are in full fellowship. He might even become an elder
someday.

This hypothetical story could be real. A lot stranger things are happening in the
twentieth century church. Human sympathy does not give Divine sanction.
Time does not change the consequence of sin for which there has been no
repentance. There is no excuse for rebelling against the will of God.

Immorality must not be tolerated in the fellowship of the church. It
desecrates its holiness. It compromises its teachings. It corrupts its members.
It destroys its influence.

The Undisciplined

The church is not to retain in its fellowship those who refuse to be
corrected from their error or repent of their sin. Jesus Himself gave this
instruction during His personal ministry.

And if your brother sins, go and reprove him in private;
if he listens to you, you have won your brother. But if
he does not listen to you, take one of two more with
you, so that BY THE MOUTH OF TWO OR THREE
WITNESSES EVERY FACT MAY BE CONFIRMED. And if he
refuses to listen to them, tell it to the church; and if
he refuses to listen even to the church, let him be to
you as a Gentile and a tax-gatherer.[49]

The magnitude of the correction is increased with every step in the process. First, there was personal confrontation. Second, there was confrontation before witnesses. Third, there was confrontation by the church. Fourth, there was rejection by the church for the one who refused to be corrected. Such a one cannot know the fellowship of the church.

If one refuses to be disciplined by the church, his original sin is compounded by others. He retaliates in anger. He tries to hurt and destroy those who "loved him enough to correct." He develops a persecution complex. It is easier to feel persecuted than it is to repent. He tries to build a party to support him in his sin and brings schism into the church.

One is reproved by the church because of the genuine care that those in the fellowship have for him. Only those who have brotherly love can care enough to correct. Only this kind of love would cause one to take the risk of confronting a brother with something he does not want to hear. Discipline is a proof of brotherly love. Such is the message of Jesus to the church in Laodicea.

Those whom I love, I reprove and discipline; be zealous therefore, and repent.[50]

When a brother is corrected by the church, it should not lead to resentment. It should rather lead to repentance. If repentance does not come, then fellowship must be broken.

This is the most painful act of love to be found in the church. One lays all that "fellowship in Christ" means on the table and risks it in one ultimate attempt to recall a brother from sin. It is an action taken as a last resort when all else fails.

If this last resort fails, there is nothing left but to refuse fellowship to the erring brother. He has rejected discipline — the supreme act of a loving fellowship. In this rejection he has cut himself off from his brothers. By doing this he has cut himself off from God. It is impossible to have fellowship with God and not be in fellowship with His children.

Conclusion

The fellowship of the church is exclusive. Were it not, then it would be without meaning.

No matter how much God desires all to be saved, some will not be. No matter how much one might want everybody to enjoy the fellowship of the body of Christ, some will be excluded. This exclusion is not determined by cultural norms or personal whims. It is determined by the plain and direct teachings of the Scriptures. The limits of fellowship are determined by God, not man.

The exclusiveness of churches of Christ is not a matter of desiring alienation from man. It is rather a matter of maintaining allegiance to Christ. If the limits of fellowship decreed by God are compromised, then the church will be no more than another human denomination.

Chart #5 The limits of fellowship "in Christ" have been set by God. Man does not determine them. He only recognizes what God has already determined. Exclusion from fellowship in Christ has nothing to do with personality, ethnic background, economic circumstances or social standing. It has everything to do with loyalty to Jesus and His teachings.

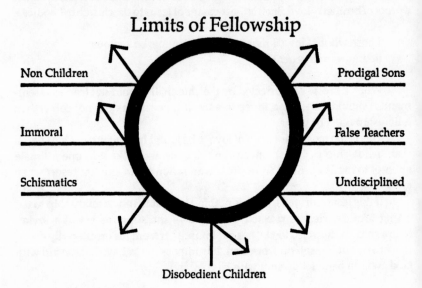

Limits of Fellowship

Non Children

Prodigal Sons

Immoral

False Teachers

Schismatics

Undisciplined

Disobedient Children

"If any one comes to you and does not bring this teaching, do not receive him into your house and do not give him a greeting; for the one who gives him a greeting participates in his evil deeds."
— II John 10-11.

Endnotes

[1] I John 1:7-9.
[2] I John 2:19.
[3] See pages 13-15.
[4] II Peter 3:9.
[5] Matthew 7:21-22.
[6] See pages 12-13.
[7] Matthew 7:21-22. See also pages 67-69.
[8] John 15:2, 4, 5-6.
[9] I John 2:19.
[10] II Thessalonians 3:6, 14.
[11] II Thessalonians 3:7-13.
[12] Discussion of the *paraousia* is in every chapter of both epistles to the Thessalonians.
[13] II Thessalonians 3:10b.
[14] II Thessalonians 3:6.
[15] II Thessalonians 3:7, 10.
[16] II Thessalonians 2:15.
[17] The word translated "tradition" is *paradosis* and refers to that which has been handed down from one group to another or from one generation to another. It is a general word which refers to both good and bad things. The Scriptures are negative about following the traditions of *men* instead of the commandments of God. (See Colossians 2:8.) The Scriptures are positive about following the traditions *coming from apostolic authority* . (See II Thessalonians 2:15; 3:6-15.) Technical words — *received* and *delivered* — are used in the New Testament indicating the process of "handing down" traditions. (See I Corinthians 11:23; 15:1-3.)
[18] Matthew 15:3, 6.
[19] II Thessalonians 3:6.
[20] II Timothy 2:17-18.
[21] II John 9-11. See pages 25-26, footnote # 22 on pages 29-31.
[22] Galatians 1:6-8.
[23] Acts 20:30.
[24] Galatians 4:16.
[25] II Thessalonians 3:15.
[26] Winfred Ernest Garrison, *The Quest and Character of a United Church* (New York: Abingdon Press, 1957), p. 6.
[27] See pages 25-26, footnote # 22 on pages 29-31 for a discussion of this passage.

[28]I John 2:3-6 and II John 6 show that the false teachers John refuted not only denied that Jesus came in the flesh but also denied the importance of commandment keeping.
[29]James 2:19.
[30]Matthew 7:21-22.
[31]I John 2:3-5.
[32]I Corinthians 1:10-17.
[33]Acts 20:28-31.
[34]The KJV uses the word "mark" in Romans 16:17 to show how the church was to regard those who cause divisions.
[35]Romans 16:17-18.
[36]Titus 3:10-11.
[37]Jude 12-13, 16, 19.
[38]It would appear that the false teachers of Jude are similar, if not identical, with those described in II Peter 2:1-22. It is interesting to note that, unlike Paul's instructions for the church to cut off the schismatics, the emphasis is upon God's final judgment upon them.
[39]I Corinthians 3:16; I Peter 2:9-10.
[40]II Corinthians 6:14-15.
[41]II Corinthians 6:16-17; 7:1. It should be noted in this passage which strings together several Old Testament quotations, there are references to Solomon's temple, Ezra's temple, and Ezekiel's ideal temple.
[42]I Corinthians 6:18-20.
[43]The word translated saints is *hagios*. Such describes those who have been sanctified or "made holy" by God. Paul argues that sexual immoralality has no place in the life of a Christian because he has been sanctified. See I Corinthians 6:9-11.
[44]Ephesians 5:3, 5, 7, 11.
[45]I Corinthians 5:4-5, 11, 13.
[46]I Corinthians 5:5.
[47]I Corinthians 5:6-8.
[48]I Corinthians 5:6.
[49]Matthew 18:15-17.
[50]Revelation 3:19.

Study Questions

1. Discuss the following statements: "One does not choose his brother. He can only recognize him as a brother when God recognizes him as a son."

2. What does it mean to be a brother in Christ?

3. Discuss each of the following groups in relationship to fellowship:

A. Non-children

B. Prodigal sons

C. Disobedient children

D. False teachers

E. Schismatics

F. The immoral

G. The undisciplined

4. Discuss the following statement: "The basis of Christian fellowship does not rest with inherited genes, academic ability, ethnic origins or economic status."

6. What is the basis of recognition of fellowship?

7. What does it mean to be a part of the family of God? What is implied in such a statement.

8. Discuss the axiom, "nothing should be made a test of fellowship which is not a condition of salvation."

9. When is a person considered a prodigal son? How should that person be treated?

10. Is there any difference between fellowship and brotherhood?

11. What is meant by christianity as both inclusive and exclusive?

12. What is the criteria for Christian fellowship?

13. How are schismatics to be treated?

14. What is the practical result of not practicing discipline in the local church?

Section 3
The Need of
Fellowship

Section I examined the nature of fellowship as shown through definitions of New Testament terms and the practice of the early church. Section II examined the scope of fellowship by showing its theological basis and defining its limits.

Section III will focus on the individual need of fellowship in living an abundant life. It will show that one can only have a full life when he has overcome loneliness, immaturity and selfishness. Fellowship in Christ is the place where one can receive motivation and help in this task.

Fellowship in Christ meets an individual's basic needs. Without these needs being met, a person will find himself empty and incomplete. There are two inadequate ways that a person will try to deal with this emptiness. On one hand he will retreat into despair and build a wall around his own loneliness. On the other hand he will seek one of the many humanistic substitutes for fellowship such as materialism, cultism and hedonism.

Fellowship fills basic human needs. Man is a social being. He both desires and needs relationships in community. It is not good for man to be alone.

> Two are better than one because they have a good return for their labor. For if either of them falls, the one will lift up his companion. But woe to the one who falls when there is not another to lift him up. Furthermore, if two lie down together they keep warm, but how can one be warm alone? And if one can overpower him who is alone, two can resist him. A cord of three strands is not quickly torn apart.[1]

Fellowship is essential to spiritual maturity. One cannot live the Christian life by himself. God desires that His people live in community. The meditative life of isolation sought by ancient monks was at best a devil's delusion. Rejection of Christian fellowship is more often a retreat from responsibility. One cannot live the Christian life without fellowship any more than members of the human body can live when they are severed from one another.

Fellowship is essential in order to have a source and object of brotherly love. Such brotherly love is the mark of being a disciple of Jesus Christ.[2] Such brotherly love is a test of of one's love for God.[3] Such brotherly love is the evidence that one has "passed out of death into life."[4] Such brotherly love can only exist if there is a brother to love.

Endnotes

[1]Ecclesiastes 4:9-12.
[2]John 13:35.
[3]I John 4:20-21.
[4]I John 3:14.

110

8/ A Place of Security

> *"In this family he is accepted with all his weaknesses and warts and is therefore willing to take the risk of openness."*

A Place to Be

Fellowship is a place to be. It is a sphere of spiritual existence based on one's relationship to God and resulting in a relationship with all of God's children in the church. It is more than a mere experiential feeling grounded in a non-rational emotionalism. It is based on a real knowledge grounded in actual obedience which can be tested by objective standards. In the context of refuting the subjectivism of pre-gnosticism, John describes these standards:

> And by this we know that we have come to know Him,
> if we keep His commandments. The one who says, "I have
> come to know Him," and does not keep His commandments,
> is a liar and the truth is not in him; but whoever keeps
> His word, in him the love of God has truly been perfected.
> By this we know that we are in Him.[1]

The emphasis is on keeping "His commandments" and keeping "His word" as a basis of knowing God. To claim to know God without keeping His commandments is dishonest. John calls one who makes such claims a liar.

The validity of one's fellowship in Christ can be tested by whether he is following His word and obeying His commandments. Such can be tested by objective means.

One can critically compare what one believes with what God says in His word. This is the very thing John recommends in exposing false teachers.

> Beloved, do not believe every spirit, but test the
> spirits to see whether they are from God; because many
> false prophets have gone out into the world.[2]

One can compare a person's actual practice with what God commands in the Scriptures. If such a person has not obeyed His commandments, then he does not know God — he is not in the sphere of fellowship where God is. If he has obeyed His commandments and keeps His word, then he knows God. He can have blessed assurance. He has a spiritual existence in the place where God is. John calls this sphere of existence "walking in the light."[3] In this spiritual sphere of light dwell all who are in fellowship with God.

Fellowship in Christ is a place to be. Its basis and limits are defined in Scripture. It must not be confused with emotional delusions or the fellowships of false faiths. One can only be sure that he really knows God when he has tested his faith and practice by the objective standards revealed in "His words" and "His commandments."

It is one thing to determine the basis and scope of fellowship in theory, but another to be able to activate this teaching in the life of the church. How is the church, in a practical way, to determine who is and who is not in its fellowship?

A practice common in the New Testament church was sending letters of introduction.[4] This is reflected in both Acts and the epistles. The brethren at Ephesus wrote letters to the disciples in Achaia to introduce Apollos.[5] Paul often included recommendations of individuals in his letters to the church.[6] He wrote to Philemon and the church in his house that they should receive Onesimus into their fellowship.

> I appeal to you for my child, whom I have begotten in
> my imprisonment, Onesimus... that you should have
> him back forever. No longer as a slave, but more than

a slave, a beloved brother, especially to me, but how
much more to you, both in the flesh and in the Lord.[7]

In sending such letters of introduction, the church had the testimony from
reliable Christians who knew the facts concerning any brother seeking to enter
their fellowship.[8]

Saul did not have such a letter when he sought to associate with the
disciples at Jerusalem. The church was afraid to extend fellowship to him until
Barnabas took him to the apostles and told of his conversion at Damascus.[9]
Oral testimony took the place of a written letter in this case.

Paul used a very descriptive phrase about fellowship in describing the
sanction which James, Cephas and John gave to Barnabas and himself:

James and Cephas and John, who were reputed to be
pillars, gave to me and Barnabas the right hand of
fellowship, that we might go to the Gentiles, and they
to the circumcised.[10]

The phrase, "right hand of fellowship," seems to have had a varied background. It could perhaps convey the idea that by giving to another one's right
hand — the hand for holding a weapon — one would be giving a gesture of
peace.

Perhaps a more accurate explanation would come from understanding
this practice in the Old Testament. The Jews who had taken foreign wives in
Babylon "gave their hand" to put them away during the reform of Ezra.[11] The
practice of "giving one's hand" is further explained in an incident involving
Jehu, king of Israel. In his journey to Samaria to destroy Ahab, Jehu met
Jehonadab, the son of Rechab. In his greetings, he said, "Is your heart right, as
my heart is with your heart?" When Jehonadab responded, "It is," Jehu said:

"If it is, give me your hand." And he gave him his hand,
and he took him up to him into the chariot.[12]

The giving of one's hand involved a pledge and acknowledgement of a
kindred spirit. It meant a "participation in" and "sanction of" a person or thing.

This certainly was the idea involved in Paul and Barnabas receiving the
"right hand of fellowship." They received approval from James, Cephas and
John for what they had been preaching among the Gentiles.

Koinonia

Fellowship "in Christ" is a place where one is confident of both his relationship with God and his relationship with the church. His relationship with God can be assured because he obeys His commandments and keeps His word. His relationship with the church is affirmed by brethren who know him and can vouch for his conduct and teachings. In this fellowship one finds security.

Identity With Divinity

One feels secure in his "fellowship in Christ" because he finds his identity is with Divinity. He can have confidence and boldness in his faith because of his connection with God.

This confidence can be illustrated through a common observation most people have witnessed.

A dog is placed in a strange environment and faced with a threatening circumstance. He is "cowed" and will avoid confrontation. He might bark, but he will keep his distance. The dog's master comes on the scene. Immediately the dog becomes more aggressive. He comes close to his master and demonstrates confidence. Nothing changes on the outside, but the dog changes on the inside. He knows his master is near.

In a similar way, a Christian is confident and has assurance. He knows his master is near. He is secure because he finds his identity with Divinity.

Such security is reflected in the boldness of the early Christians. They were confident because they believed God was in their midst. Such was the observation of the Jewish council:

Now as they observed the confidence of Peter and
John, and understood that they were uneducated and
untrained men, they were marveling, and began to
recognize them as having been with Jesus.[13]

The confidence of Peter and John was due to the identity they had with Jesus. They had no basis to feel secure in their education or training, but they did in their fellowship with Jesus.

Paul relates to Timothy how "no one supported me, but all deserted me" when he appeared before the emperor at his first defense. Such did not cause his confidence to wane. He felt secure because of his fellowship with Jesus.

114

But the Lord stood with me, and strengthened me,
in order that through me the proclamation might be
fully accomplished and that all the Gentiles might
hear; and I was delivered out of the lion's mouth.[14]

The book of Hebrews was addressed to discouraged Christians who had lost their confidence. They are admonished to take courage in their relationship with God:

...being content with what you have; for He Himself
has said, "I WILL NEVER DESERT YOU, NOR WILL I EVER
FORSAKE YOU," so that we confidently say, "THE LORD
IS MY HELPER, I WILL NOT BE AFRAID. WHAT SHALL MAN
DO TO ME?"[15]

Christian confidence and security does not come from psycho-cybernetics, humanistic positive thinking, political power, economic wealth or personal ability. It comes solely and wholly from God.

The Christian recognizes that his very identity is wrapped up in the grace of God. Family name, academic acclaim and popular fame are all illusions. A Christian's real identity is in God. There are no "self-made men." Paul affirmed such in his own life. He said, "But by the grace of God I am what I am."[16]

Before Paul became a Christian he had reason for much confidence in the flesh. He was schooled under the greatest rabbi of his day, probably tutored in Greek philosophy at Tarsus and the proud possessor of Roman citizenship. He traced his ancestors through one of the finest families of Israel. He was far advanced in the Pharisee sect of the Jews. He had, it would appear, nearly everything any Jew of his day could want.

When Paul became a Christian, all of these advantages were esteemed in a different way. The only thing that was important was his relationship with God.

But whatever things were gain to me, those things I
have counted as loss for the sake of Christ. More than
that, I count all things to be loss in view of the
surpassing value of knowing Christ Jesus my Lord, for
whom I have suffered the loss of all things, and count
them but rubbish in order that I may gain Christ.[17]

The Christian recognizes that all that he is and everything he has is a "grace gift" from God. His abilities, his opportunities and his power does not come from self effort. They are gifts of God. Man is only the steward of God's grace gifts.

> As each one has received a special gift, employ it in
> serving one another, as good stewards of the manifold
> grace of God.[18]

The Christian recognizes that even his opportunity to use grace gifts comes from God. It is God who opens the doors of opportunity.[19] It is God who also hinders.[20]

It is in God that a Christian finds his identity. It is from God that he receives grace gifts. It is by God that doors of opportunity are opened. There is no room for personal glory. One must confess that, by himself, he is inadequate. He can only find confidence in God. Such was the confession of Paul:

> And such confidence we have through Christ toward God.
> Not that we are adequate in ourselves to consider
> anything as coming from ourselves, but our adequacy is
> from God.[21]

A Christian finds his identity with Divinity. This is the basis of his security and the motivation of his confidence. Without God a man is nothing. With God all things are possible.[22] This concept is well expressed in a song sung by college students in the seventies:

> Without Him I would be nothing
> Without Him I'd surely fail
> Without Him I would be drifting
> Like a ship without a sail.

A Christian finds security, not in who he is, but in whose he is.

Identity With Family

One feels secure in his "fellowship in Christ" because he is identified with the family of God. By faith in God security can be found in one's relationship with Divinity. Security can be found in the family of God through the practice of fellowship. To find a place in the world where one can say, "I belong!" brings security. To find a relationship where one is accepted for who he is — with all his warts — brings confidence.

This great blessing came to the Gentiles when the church was established. Paul described their former plight and their present blessing to the church at Ephesus:

> Therefore remember, that formerly you, the Gentiles
> in the flesh, who are called "Uncircumcision" by the
> so-called "Circumcision"...remember that you were
> at that time separate from Christ, excluded from the
> commonwealth of Israel, and strangers to the covenants
> of promise having no hope and without God in the world.
> But now in Christ Jesus you who formerly were far off
> have been brought near by the blood of Christ.[23]

The cross of Christ not only spanned the gulf of sin which separated man from God, but it also spanned the gulf of estrangement which separated man from man. This was done in the church. Paul described this new relationship in the church:

> So then you are no longer strangers and aliens, but
> you are fellow-citizens with the saints, and are of
> God's household.[24]

This relationship in the church gives security and builds confidence. Such can be demonstrated by this athletic illustration.

A basketball team was not doing well one season. They had good material and good coaching but could not get it all together to win games. The team needed to change the way they were thinking about themselves individually and as the team collectively. They did. Each player quit trying to "go it alone" and identified with the team. They encouraged and complemented one another. Things began to change. The players lost their own identity in the team effort. By this they found a team identity and gained confidence to play their best. They now had the will to win games. The team spirit — the theological term is "fellowship" — was necessary for their security and success.

It is in this family identity that one loses himself for the good of the family. He no longer thinks of the family as "they" and "them" but "we" and "us." He does not regard himself as a spectator on the sidelines but as a participant in the game. In this identity he finds security. In this identity he also finds strength and power.

It is in this family identity that one gives acceptance and finds acceptance. He is accepted with his warts and overlooks the warts of others.

The family of God is made up of redeemed sinners — nothing else. They are in the family because God gave them new life as one of His children. They gave up their sins and were born into God's family. It does not make any difference who they were or what they used to do in their old life. That is past and gone. They now are God's children and as such are connected in brotherhood with every other child of God.

This brotherhood involves mutual care for every other member of the family. When a brother is injured, the rest of the family is able to feel the pain. When a brother is honored, the rest of the family rejoices in it. When a brother is discouraged, the rest of the family gives encouragment. When a brother is overtaken in sin, the rest of the family restores him to fellowship. There is oneness in the family. Heartaches are shared. One takes the risk of confessing sins and revealing weaknesses. One becomes vulnerable by letting down his guard because he trusts his brother.

Fellowship in Christ provides a forum of caring Christians with whom he is able to share his real self. He is able to take the risk of being vulnerable with others. In this fellowship one can share his deepest doubts, highest ideals, blackest sins, most noble aspirations, most humbling weaknesses and his greatest victories. He has a community in which he can let down his guard and still find acceptance. His concern is not: "What if people really find out about me?" It is rather: "How can I be more open and honest about my needs?" In this fellowship there is forgiveness, openness, acceptance and caring confrontation.

The need for such an openness in relationships is well documented by the rise of counseling professions. People desire to open their souls to someone who really cares and understands. Psychologists and counselors are more and more filling the void which has been created by the neglect of this important part of Christian fellowship.[25] These people-helping professions certainly have their place, but they are only a counterfeit of what God intended Christian fellowship to be.

It has often been said that the popularity of the neighborhood bar can be attributed to the camaraderie of its clientel as much as to the spirits it sells. The bar flourishes not because most people are alcoholics, but because people seek a place to know and be known in a community in which one can be himself and still be accepted. Bruce Larson makes such an observation:

> The neighborhood bar is possibly the best counterfeit
> there is to the fellowship Christ wants to give His
> church. It's an imitation, dispensing liquor instead of
> grace, escape rather than reality. But it is a
> permissive, accepting, and inclusive fellowship. It is
> unshockable; it is democratic. You can tell people
> secrets and they usually don't tell others, or want to.[26]

An unknown author has penned these words which fit so well what fellowship in Christ should be.

> If this is not a place where tears are understood,
>   Where do I go to cry?
> If this is not a place where my spirit can wing,
>   Where do I go to fly?
> If this is not a place where my questions can be asked,
>   Where do I go to seek?
> If this is not a place where my feelings can be heard,
>   Where do I go to speak?
> If this is not a place where you'll accept me as I am,
>   Where do I go to be me?
> If this is not a place where I can try and fail and learn and grow,
>   Where can I be — just me?

Fellowship in Christ is a place of security. It is grounded in one's relationship with God. One can know he is in this fellowship because he keeps His word and obeys His commandments. This feeling of security gives one confidence. He is bold because he finds his identity in Divinity. This security involves one in the loving and caring family of God. In this family he is accepted with all his weaknesses and warts and is therefore willing to take the risk of openness.

Koinonia

Endnotes

¹I John 2:3-5.
²I John 4:1.
³I John 1:7.
⁴Such letters of introduction were not unique to Christians. Many such letters are to be found in the papyri. Acts 9:1-2 shows that Saul had letters from the high priest at Jerusalem to introduce him to the synagogues of Damascus.
⁵Acts 18:27.
⁶Romans 16:1-2; I Corinthians 16:10-11; II Corinthians 8:23; Ephesians 6:21-22; Colossians 4:7-8.
⁷Philemon 10, 15-16.
⁸It should be noted that such a practice was not always without abuse. II Corinthians 3:1 reveals what appears to be a case of certain teachers who were opposing Paul but who also had letters of commendation.
⁹Acts 9:26-27.
¹⁰Galatians 2:9.
¹¹Ezra 10:19. The idea of "giving one's hand" seems to imply a pledge in this context. This is reflected in most translations.
¹²II Kings 10:15.
¹³Acts 4:13.
¹⁴II Timothy 4:16-17.
¹⁵Hebrews 13:5-6. Three Old Testament passages lie behind this quotation. One is in the Law, Deuteronomy 31:6. One is in the History, Joshua 5:5. One is in the Psalms, Psalm 118:6.
¹⁶I Corinthians 15:10.
¹⁷Philippians 3:7-8.
¹⁸I Peter 4:10. It should be noted that the word translated "special gift" is *charisma* which literally means "grace gift".
¹⁹Revelation 3:8.
²⁰Acts 16:6-7.
²¹II Corinthians 3:4-5.
²²Matthew 19:26.
²³Ephesians 2:11-13.
²⁴Ephesians 2:19.
²⁵The counterfeit of psychology as religion is shown in such books as Paul C. Vitz, *Psychology as Religion* (Grand Rapids: William B. Eerdmans Pub-

120

lishing Company, 1982) and William Kirk Kilpatrick, *Psychological Seduction* (New York: Thomas Nelson Publishers, 1983).
[26]Bruce Larson, *Dare to Live Now!* (Grand Rapids: Zondervan, n.d), p. 110.

Study Questions

1. Discuss fellowship as a place of security in the family of God.

2. Is there a real basis for appealing to passages of scripture as they relate to a person's practice?

3. How is fellowship related to an identity with Divinity?

4. How does identity relate to others within the fellowship?

5. How is identity related to the family (in the church)?

6. A proper "team spirit" for a basketball team was used to illustrate the concept of fellowship. Can you think of other examples?

7. How does proper fellowship produce confidence in serving Christ?

8. Discuss the importance of security found in fellowship.

9. Discuss how "fellowship in Christ" finds identity with Divinity.

10. How does identity with family relate to fellowship in Christ?

9/ *A Place of Growth*

"There is strength in community."
"No longer must one feel alone and isolated."
"He has the assurance of Divine help."

The Need of Community

Fellowship in Christ is a place where one can grow. One cannot attain spiritual maturity or even survive without the nurture that comes from being in the church. Man is by nature a social being. He is influenced by those with whom he associates.

If his associations are good, he will become stronger. If they are bad, he will grow weaker. This is the reason the Scriptures encourage a Christian to be selective in his choice of relationships.

Do not be deceived: Bad company corrupts good morals.[1]

Do not be bound together with unbelievers; for what

partnership have righteousness and lawlessness, or what
fellowship has light with darkness? Or what harmony
has Christ with Belial, or what has a believer in common
with an unbeliever?... "Therefore, COME OUT FROM
THEIR MIDST AND BE SEPARATE," says the Lord.
"AND DO NOT TOUCH WHAT IS UNCLEAN."[2]

One's association cannot help but have an influence on his attitudes and
values. If one is to attain spiritual growth, he must choose relationships that
will make it possible. One cannot grow spiritually by isolation from fellowship
in Christ. One cannot grow spiritually when he is surrounded by corrupting
influences of immorality, humanism and unbelievers. Fellowship in Christ is
a place in which spiritual growth can take place.

There is strength in community. This is evident from the experiences of
life. If one desires to maintain a program of exercise for bodily health, he will
find it easier to do it in community. If one desires to go on a diet, he will find
it is easier to do it in community. The encouragement and discipline which are
found in a community effort are far more efficient than trying to "go it alone."

The work of Alcoholics Anonymous is only possible because of the
mutual help members give to and receive from one another in the organization. They have learned the strength of community. This is expressed in the
A.A. Tradition:

...no society of men and women had a more urgent
need for continuous effectiveness and permanent unity.
We alcoholics see that we must work together and hang
together, else most of us will finally die alone.[3]

They have learned that one can help himself only by helping others. The first
of the twelve traditions in A.A. centers upon helping one another:

Our A.A. experience has taught us that: 1. Each
member of Alcoholics Anonymous is but a small part
of a great whole. A.A. must continue to live or most
of us will surely die. Hence our common welfare
comes first.[4]

A neurologist, Dr. Foster Kennedy, makes this observation about the communal power of A.A.:

This organization of Alcoholics Anonymous calls on
two of the greatest reservoirs of power known to man,
religion and that instinct for association with one's
fellow... the "herd instinct." I think our profession
must take appreciative cognizance of this great
therapeutic weapon.[5]

One cannot minimize the influence of group dynamics in changing the values, morals and lifestyle of the individual. The group, by its very nature, brings about change in anyone who is in it. There are group models that become patterns. There is group pressure to conform. There is group encouragement to motivate. There is group confrontation to discipline. The dynamics of group interaction are neutral. They can be either good or bad — depending on the group.

These laws of group dynamics experienced in all social groups are only a part of the power of fellowship in Christ.

The bond that binds together those in fellowship with Christ is stronger than that of other groups. That tie is the Holy Spirit who dwells in every Christian and in the church itself.[6] It is a spiritual and eternal tie greater and more powerful than any earthly tie. The strength of this tie makes fellowship in Christ the place of spiritual growth.

Those involved in fellowship in Christ have greater motivation for growth than exists in other groups whose motivation is centered in better health, stronger bodies or even living a sober life. These motives are good and noble, but they are not nearly as powerful as those that motivate Christians. Christians are motivated by love for their Lord.[7] They are motivated by a desire for eternal life.[8] Their motivation is greater than human relationships and higher than this world. Such is described in a little tract published by the Herald of Truth:

Before He left the earth, Jesus established the support
group He knew I would need. In His divine wisdom, He
established His church as a fellowship of those... like
me... who are being saved by their belief in Him. He
knows the fragile nature of my faith... and the
awesome power of life's temptations, so He gives me
a world-wide network of brothers and sisters in His
love... a church family to support my new life in Him.[9]

Koinonia

Fellowship in Christ demands a greater commitment than any other commitment in life. It involves a total surrender to the will of God. Nothing else has priority over it. There must be a willingness to sacrifice all things for it. Jesus expressed the demands of this commitment in His personal ministry.

If anyone comes to Me, and does not hate his own
father and mother and wife and children and brothers
and sisters, yes, and even his own life, he cannot be My
disciple. Whoever does not carry his own cross and
come after Me cannot be My disciple... So therefore,
no one of you can be My disciple who does not give up
all his own possessions.[10]

This commitment to Christ and His church supercedes all other commitments. When such a commitment exists in a fellowship, it becomes a place of spiritual growth.

Fellowship in Christ is a place where barriers of spiritual growth are overcome. No longer must one feel alone and isolated. He has found identity with and support from others like himself. No longer does he have to feel self-sufficient and act independently. He is part of a fellowship that cares and shares. They help him to bear his burdens and give him support in his goals.

Fellowship Terms Promoting Growth

The epistles of the New Testament are filled with exhortations for spiritual growth.[11] This spiritual growth was to be accomplished in community. Each member of Christ's body, the Church, was connected to and had responsibility for every other member.

Brethren, even if a man is caught in any trespass,
you who are spiritual, restore such a one in a spirit
of gentleness; looking to yourself, lest you too be
tempted. Bear one another's burdens, and thus fulfill
the law of Christ.[12]

My brethren, if any among you strays from the truth, and
one turns him back; let him know that he who turns a
sinner from the error of his way will save his soul from
death, and will cover a multitude of sins.[13]

126

Brotherhood — fellowship in Christ — carries with it the responsibility of promoting growth in God's other children. It is the law of Christ.

A number of different terms are used in Scripture describing the way one is to aid his brother in spiritual growth. Notice the different verbs Paul used to instruct the church at Thessalonica:

> And we urge you, brethren, *admonish* the unruly,
> *encourage* the fainthearted, *help* the weak, *be*
> *patient* with all men.[14]

It would appear that these terms reflect different kinds of problems causing spiritual immaturity. Each of these terms involves a person-to-person confrontation. In fact, the correction has much more power because it is a personal confrontation from one who shares in a fellowship in Christ.

Some are to be taught. They are ignorant of the error of their faith or the wrongness of their conduct. They need instruction in truth. Such was the case of Apollos in Ephesus. He was ignorant of Jesus, "being acquainted only with the baptism of John." Priscilla and Aquila "took him aside and explained to him the way of God more accurately."[15]

Some are to be exhorted. They have become discouraged and depressed because of persecution, disappointments with others, and their own failure in living the Christian life. This has led to weakness in their faith and neglect in their conduct. Such a condition is descriptive of the second and third generation Christians to whom the epistle to the Hebrews is addressed.

> Therefore, strengthen the hands that are weak and the
> knees that are feeble, and make straight paths for your
> feet, so that the limb which is lame may not be put out
> of joint, but rather be healed.[16]

Exhortation is the theme of Hebrews. It was written to discouraged Christians who were in danger of falling away. They are admonished to:

> ...encourage one another day after day, as long as
> it is still called "Today," lest any one of you be
> hardened by the deceitfulness of sin.[17]

Some are to be reproved. Reproof is one of the tasks of an evangelist.[18] It is the kind of action that is to be taken when a brother is trying to get others to participate in sin. Such was the case in Ephesus:

127

And do not participate in the unfruitful deeds of
darkness, but instead even expose them; for it is
disgraceful even to speak of the things which are
done by them in secret.[19]

It would appear that reproof is given to those who should know better but are
still involved in sin.

Some are to be rebuked. Such strong action is taken against those who
rebel against the teachings of Christ and in so doing are leading others astray.
Such was the case of Peter at Antioch. He knew that "God was no respecter of
persons," but because of pressure from the brethren who came from Judea, he
refused to eat with Gentiles. This led Barnabas and others to withdraw
themselves from the fellowship of the Gentile brethren. Paul rebuked him to
his face.[20] Later Paul was to instruct Timothy to publicly rebuke those who
"continue in sin" in order that "the rest also may be fearful of sinning."[21]

Some are to be admonished or warned. Such is to be done to those who
are unruly.[22] It appears that such a warning is a final effort to correct those who
are unruly or undisciplined in the church. In I Thessalonians brethren are told
to "admonish" the unruly and in II Thessalonians the brethren are told to
"keep aloof from every brother who leads an unruly life."[23]

Prayers are to be given for brethren who sin. The only exception to this
is the "sin leading to death."[24] Simon asked Peter to pray for him when he was
convicted of his sin.[25] One of the most beautiful expressions of fellowship in
Christ is found in James where brethren are told to confess their sins to one
another and pray for one another.

Therefore, confess your sins to one another, and pray for
one another, so that you may be healed. The effective
prayer of a righteous man can accomplish much.[26]

Some are to be cast to Satan. When a brother refuses to repent of his sin,
he is to be cast to Satan. Such was the case of the immoral brother at Corinth.[27]
When a brother refuses to quit teaching false doctrine, he is to be cast to Satan.[28]
The purpose of such action is not vindictive but remedial.

I have decided to deliver such a one to Satan for the
destruction of his flesh, that his spirit may be saved
in the day of the Lord Jesus.[29]

Casting to Satan is the last resort for saving a brother involved in sin and error. It can be effective only if the fellowship of the church is strong enough to break the heart which has been hardened by sin. If fellowship in Christ means nothing to the corrected brother, then such will not lead him to repentance.

These seven terms aptly describe the kind of action which is involved in the church to help each individual member attain spiritual growth. The action involved in these terms will only be as effective as the fellowship is strong.

Special Help in Growth

Fellowship in Christ is a place in which one receives special help in Christian growth. It is easier to live a righteous life in the church — the place of fellowship in Christ — than it is in the world. It is foolish for a person to reason that he will first conquer his sins and then he will become a Christian. One cannot do such alone. He needs the power of God and the help of the brethren to conquer sin in his life. When one becomes a Christian, he immediately has advantages he has never had before. He has help for both conquering sin and obtaining spiritual growth.

He has a new relationship with God by which he can call Him "Abba, Father."[30] His prayers are more effective. He has the promise of God's providential care.[31] He has the assurance of Divine help:

No temptation has overtaken you but such as is
common to man; and God is faithful, who will not
allow you to be tempted beyond what you are able,
but with the temptation will provide the way of
escape also, that you may be able to endure it.[32]

He has a friend and helper in Jesus Christ. One who is in fellowship in Christ has a sympathetic high priest who pleads on his behalf before the throne of God when he prays.[33] Jesus understands the plight of man because He became man. Jesus sits on the right hand of the throne of God and has full access to the Father. Such a one can indeed be a perfect mediator.[34] One who is in fellowship in Christ has power to accomplish that which he could not do by himself.

Christ stood by Paul when he appeared before the emperor.[35] This gave him confidence. Christ was on his side, and he was not afraid. Christ is the Christian's helper in time of need and his strength in time of fear. Paul was speaking of the confidence he had in Christ's help when he wrote the following:

I can do all things through Him who strengthens me.[36]

He has a comforter and helper in the Holy Spirit. The Holy Spirit who dwells in the Christian aids him in his prayers.[37] He helps him to overcome opposition in the world.[38] He is the tie that binds one to God and to all of God's other children. Paul wrote of this help of the Holy Spirit in his letter to the Ephesians:

Now to Him who is able to do exceeding abundantly
beyond all that we ask or think, according to the power
that works within us...[39]

Fellowship in Christ is the place of spiritual growth because one has the help of God, Christ and the Holy Spirit.

It is easier for one who knows fellowship in Christ to live a righteous life because he has the help of brethren.

When one becomes a Christian, he becomes a part of a holy people and dwells in God's holy temple, the church. This holiness is a motivation to live above sin. As a part of God's holy people one seeks to lead a holy life.

Fellowship in Christ means one is part of a caring community. One finds his identity in this community. He finds a sense of belonging in this community. He finds a community who cares about him and for him. He even finds a community of believers who are so concerned about his spiritual welfare that they do not hesitate to confront him if he goes astray.

Fellowship in Christ — in His church — is the place where one can attain spiritual growth and maturity.

Endnotes

[1]I Corinthians 15:33.
[2]II Corinthians 6:14-15, 17.
[3]_____, *Alcoholics Anonymous* (New York City: Alcoholics Anonymous World Service, Inc., 1988), p. 563.
[4]*op. cit.* p. 565.
[5]*op. cit.*, p. 571.
[6]Paul argues against fornication by affirming that the Christian's body is the temple of the Holy Spirit in I Corinthians 6:19. Paul argues against church division by affirming that the church is the temple of the Holy Spirit in

I Corinthians 3:16.
⁷II Coirinthians 5:14-15.
⁸II Corinthians 5:1-4.
⁹_____, *Jesus and His Church* (Abilene: Herald of Truth, 1988), p. 3.
¹⁰Luke 14:26-27, 33.
¹¹Peter exhorts the brethren to grow in both of his epistles. (See I Peter 2:2 and II Peter 3:18.) Paul both reproves the Corinthians because of their lack of growth and encourages them to mature. (See I Corinthians 3:1-2 and I Corinthians 14:20.) The Hebrews are reproved for their spiritual immaturity. (See Hebrews 5:11-14.)
¹²Galatians 6:1-2.
¹³James 5:19-20.
¹⁴I Thessalonians 5:14.
¹⁵Acts 18:25-26.
¹⁶Hebrews 12:12-13.
¹⁷Hebrews 3:13.
¹⁸II Timothy 4:2.
¹⁹Ephesians 5:11-12. An alternate reading for "expose" in verse 11 is "reprove".
²⁰Galatians 2:11-13.
²¹I Timothy 5:20.
²²I Thessalonians 5:14.
²³II Thessalonians 3:6-7.
²⁴I John 5:16.
²⁵Acts 8:22-24.
²⁶James 5:16.
²⁷I Corinthians 5:1-13. See pages 99-102 for a discussion of such discipline.
²⁸I Timothy 1:20; II Timothy 2:17-18.
²⁹I Corinthians 5:5.
³⁰Galatians 4:6.
³¹Romans 8:28.
³²I Corinthians 10:13.
³³Hebrews 4:14-16.
³⁴I Timothy 2:5.
³⁵II Timothy 4:17.
³⁶Philippians 4:13.
³⁷Romans 8:26.
³⁸I John 4:4.
³⁹Ephesians 3:20.

Study Questions

1. Discuss how a "need for community" is important in understanding the importance of fellowship.

2. Discuss each of the terms used in this chapter under the heading "Fellowship Terms Promoting Growth."

3. Discuss the relationship of "bad company" with the idea of fellowship in the body.

4. What part does fellowship play in helping spiritual growth?

5. Is it possible that the tie that binds Christians together can be stronger than any other ties on earth? Discuss.

6. What are some of the motivations for growth within the body of Christ and how is this related to fellowship?

7. Does brotherhood carry with it the responsibility of promoting growth in other of God's children? Discuss.

8. What part does rebuking and admonishing play in fellowship within the body of Christ?

9. Discuss the kind of love needed to practice discipline within the church.

10 / A Place of Love

> "One cannot be a Christ lover and a church hater."
>
> "It is a willed love which is not dependent upon the object of love being lovable or worthy. "

Proof of Discipleship

Fellowship in Christ is perhaps best described as a place of love. Love is the cement that binds followers of Christ together. In the context of being "born again," Peter exhorted Christians to practice brotherly love as a natural outflowing of their new birth:

> Since you have in obedience to the truth purified
> your souls for a sincere love of the brethren, fervently
> love one another from the heart.[1]

Love is the symbol by which the world is able to recognize the disciples of Christ. It is the "mark of identity" for the church of Christ. It is the way to prove to the world that those who claim to follow Jesus are really sincere. Jesus Himself taught this:

A new commandment I give to you, that you love one
another, even as I have loved you, that you also love
one another. By this all men will know that you are
My disciples, if you have love for one another.[2]

Love is the only basis by which fellowship in Christ can exist. Without
brotherly love it would be impossible to bridge the chasms of differences
which naturally exist between the followers of Christ.

In a theological way, barriers between men were broken down at the
cross. This is expressed by Paul in discussing how Jews and Gentiles became
one in Christ:

For He Himself is our peace, who made both groups into
one, and broke down the barrier of the dividing wall, by
abolishing in His flesh the enmity, which is the Law of
commandments contained in ordinances, that in Himself
He might make two into one new man, thus establishing
peace, and might reconcile them both in one body to God
through the cross...[3]

In a practical way, barriers between men are broken down by brotherly love
in the church. Fellowship in Christ can exist only when it finds expression in
agape love.

This kind of love is more than an emotional feeling, an erotic urge, a
family identity or a closeness based on friendship. It finds its origin in the heart
of the giver. It exists regardless of how undesirable the object of love might be.
It has everything to do with the subject and nothing to do with the object. It is
a love that has been commanded and therefore can be willed. God does not
give impossible commandments. It is this kind of love that is necessary for
fellowship in Christ.

It is this brotherly love that makes it possible for people from diverse
backgrounds, varied interests, different levels of culture and economic status
to be bound together in fellowship. Such a union can only exist when it is
motivated by brotherly love.

A song sung by university students expresses the means of brotherhood
in the family of God:

Bind us together Lord, Bind us together Lord,
  With chains which cannot be broken,

Bind us together Lord, Bind us together Lord
Bind us together in love.

There is only one Lord,
There is only one king,
There is only one body,
And that is why we can sing.

Bind us together Lord, Bind us together Lord,
With chains which cannot be broken.
Bind us together Lord, Bind us together Lord,
Bind us together in love.[4]

Erick Fromm writes of ways by which individuals seek to escape "separateness" in the world. He shows how men seek unity with others in four different states. The first state is orgiastic unity achieved by drugs, religious ritual and the sexual experience. The second state is conformity unity achieved through yielding to customs, practices and beliefs of a state, culture or cult. An equality is achieved through sameness rather than oneness, but there is the loss of individuality. The third state is achieved by creative activity that might bring an artist and his art together to find a kind of identity, but such is impersonal. After discussing the failure of these methods of seeking unity, Fromm writes:

> The unity achieved in productive work is not
> interpersonal; the unity achieved in orgiastic fusion
> is transitory; the unity achieved by conformity is only
> pseudo-unity. Hence, they are only partial answers to
> the problem of existence. The full answer lies in the
> achievement of interpersonal union, of fusion with
> another person, in love.[5]

From a strictly humanistic vantage point Fromm shows the importance of love in uniting people. Much more can one see such love bringing about fellowship when it is motivated by one's faith in Christ.

Giving and Receiving

Fellowship in Christ is a place of giving and receiving in brotherly love. As already noted, the meaning of the word "fellowship" involves a sharing.[6] This meaning, according to Luke, found expression in the church after Pentecost.

> And all those who had believed were together, and
> had all things in common.[7]

> And the congregation of those who believed were of
> one heart and soul; and not one of them claimed that
> anything belonging to him was his own; but all things
> were common property to them.[8]

One of the English words which is used to translate *koinonia* is "contribution." It is so translated with reference to the contribution given by the church at Corinth to the saints in Jerusalem.[9]

Giving is so much a part of fellowship that Paul says it is a proof of brotherly love.

> Therefore openly before the churches show them the
> proof of your love and of our reason for boasting
> about you.[10]

Giving is so much a part of fellowship in Christ that to neglect it is to deny one's love of God.

> We know love by this, that He laid down His life for us;
> and we ought to lay down our lives for the brethren.
> But whoever has the world's goods , and beholds his
> brother in need and closes his heart against him, how
> does the love of God abide in him?[11]

Fellowship in Christ involves the ability "to receive with thanksgiving" as much as it involves the ability "to give with unselfishness." Paul speaks of both giving and receiving as a part of fellowship in his "thank you" letter to the church at Philippi:

And you yourselves also know, Philippians, that at the
first preaching of the gospel, after I departed from
Macedonia, no church shared with me in the matter of
giving and receiving but you alone.[12]

The sharing involved both giving and receiving. The word translated "shared"
— *ekoinonesen* — is a fellowship word. Fellowship in Christ involved the
church at Phillipi giving a contribution to Paul. It also involved Paul receiving
it with thanksgiving. This is what the letter to Philippi was all about. Paul was
participating in fellowship by saying "thank you."

But I have received everything in full, and have an
abundance; I am amply supplied, having received from
Epaphroditus what you have sent, a fragrant aroma, an
acceptable sacrifice, well pleasing to God.[13]

Fellowship in Christ is a place of love in which both giving and receiving
abound.

Brotherly Love

A much neglected command in the church is "love the brotherhood!"[14]
Sometimes the worldwide brotherhood of the church is taken for granted. One
is only concerned with his own little circle of Christians within his own
community.

Sometimes the brotherhood is despised. One only sees its human weaknesses and is able to hear only of its failings. He does not want to be identified
with it.

Sometimes the brotherhood is not very lovable. Those in the brotherhood
say foolish things and act in selfish ways. One experiences the feelings of
frustration and shame.

It then becomes evident that brotherly love is only possible if it is *agape*
love. This is the kind of willed love that God had for unlovable man. This is the
kind of unselfish love Jesus demonstrated on the cross. It is only by this kind
of love that one can love the brotherhood and the brotherhood can love me.

Jesus commanded "neighbor love" as a part of the all encompassing great
commandment.[15] He illustrated it with the story of the Good Samaritan.[16] It
involved compassion.

Jesus commanded "enemy love" in contrast with the false teachings of the rabbi who taught:

...You SHALL LOVE YOUR NEIGHBOR, AND HATE YOUR ENEMY.[17]

He illustrated love of enemy with the love that God has for all men—good and bad, righteous and unrighteous. This is a love which is kind to all men without regard for evil which they have done.

Jesus commanded "brother love," which he said would be the badge of discipleship. In spite of the fact that he had already given commands to "love your enemy" and "love your neighbor," he called the command for His disciples to love one another a "new commandment." How was it new?

It had a new motive. It was not a love of duty as much as it was a reflection of the love that God and Christ had for man. This is shown in John's first epistle:

...He laid down His life for us; and we ought to lay down our lives for the brethren.[18]

By this the love of God was manifested in us, that God has sent His only begotten Son into the world so that we might live through Him... Beloved, if God so loved us, we also ought to love one another.[19]

It had a new object. It was more than compassion for a neighbor and kindness toward an enemy. It involved those who were Jesus' disciples, children of God — brethren. One cannot be a Christ lover and a church hater. He cannot be a brother hater and a God lover. Such is a contradiction and hypocrisy.

If someone says, "I love God," and hates his brother, he is a liar; for the one who does not love his brother whom he has seen, cannot love God whom he has not seen. And this commandment we have from Him, that the one who loves God should love his brother also.[20]

It had a new magnitude. Such was expressed clearly when the new commandment was given. The love for one another was to be "as I have loved you."[21] Jesus loved man when he was unlovable. Even though man was defiled by sin, rebelled against God and despised holiness, Jesus loved him. Jesus loved man when he was unworthy and did not merit it. Even though he was hopelessly lost in sin, helplessly weak and even an enemy of God, Jesus loved him.[22] Jesus loved man sacrificially. He left his home in heaven. He cast off his Divine nature to such a degree that he was tempted to sin, suffered in the flesh and died on the cross. He emptied Himself in total and complete unselfishness. His love shows how brothers in Christ are to love one another.

It had a new purpose. It was to be the badge of discipleship. It was to reflect to the world that those who practiced this kind of love were followers of Jesus Christ.

Neglect of brotherly love is a damnable sin. One will never see heaven unless he learns to love his brother.

This is shown in the parable of the sheep and goats. The parable is about the final judgment God brings upon men. Some will "inherit the kingdom" and others will be cast "into eternal fire." The basis of the judgment in this parable is whether or not a person has shown love to his brothers:

Then He will also say to those on His left, "Depart from Me, accursed ones, into eternal fire which has been prepared for the devil and his angels; for I was hungry, and you gave Me nothing to eat; I was thirsty, and you gave Me nothing to drink; I was a stranger, and you did not invite Me in; naked, and you did not clothe Me; sick, and in prison, and you did not visit Me." Then they themselves also will answer, saying, "Lord when did we see You hungry, or thirsty, or a stranger, or naked, or sick, or in prison, and did not take care of You?" Then He will answer them, saying, Truly I say to you, to the extent that you did not do it to one of the least of these, you did not do it to Me." And these will go away into eternal punishment, but the righteous into eternal life.[23]

The parable clearly shows that God does not tolerate the neglect of brotherly love among His children.

The neglect of brotherly love is shown in the parable of the prodigal son.[24] The whole point of the parable was to expose the sinful pride of the scribes and Pharisees who condemned Jesus for receiving tax collectors and sinners. The villain of the parable is not the prodigal son but the elder brother. He depicts the unmerciful attitude of the scribes and Pharisees. The love of the Father never waned for the prodigal son but the elder brother refused to show brotherly love. He would not rejoice on the return of his wayward brother. He was jealous of the attention which the Father gave to his lost son. He had no mercy, no forgiveness, no compassion and certainly no brotherly love.

Fellowship in Christ is the place that brotherly love abounds. In the practical section of Romans, Paul gives this clear admonition:

> Be devoted to one another in brotherly love; give
> preference to one another in honor.[25]

Description of Brotherly Love

If fellowship in Christ is a place of brotherly love, then a description would be helpful in learning how to practice it. Using the structure of Paul's description of *agape* love in I Corinthians 13, one might suggest the following:

> Love is patient — and allows time for a brother to mature.

> Love is kind — even when a brother is unkind.

> Love is not jealous — even if a brother has something
> he does not have.

> Love does not brag — even if one has something that his
> brother does not have.

> Love is not arrogant — but esteems his brother better
> than himself.

> Love does not act unbecomingly — for there is never a reason
> to be rude, crude and inconsiderate to a brother.

> Love does not seek its own — but looks out for the
> interest of his brother.

> Love is not provoked — but turns the other cheek and
> goes the second mile.

Love does not take account of wrong suffered — and forgets the bad and the ugly which he has suffered without trying to get even.

Love does not rejoice in unrighteousness — for he does not like to hear of bad things happening even to an evil person.

Love bears all things — and delights in taking the heaviest load, the dirtiest job and the short end of the stick.

Love believes all things — even when a brother has disappointed him in the past and he has lost faith in himself.

Love hopes all things — even if things looks bad he continues to hope against all odds.

Love endures all things — even when it means heart break, injustice and betrayal.

Love never fails — even when a brother is obnoxious, cranky, unlovable and mean.

Fellowship in Christ is the place of brotherly love. The love expressed in this fellowship is a demonstration of the love Jesus had for the world. It is a willed love which is not dependent upon the object of love being lovable or worthy. It is a love that finds expression in unselfish service. No wonder the last chapter of Hebrews begins with an admonition for such a love to continue:

Let love of the brethren continue. Do not neglect to show hospitality to strangers, for by this some have entertained angels without knowing it. Remember the prisoners, as though in prison with them; and those who are ill-treated, since you yourselves also are in the body.[26]

The "will to" and the "practice of" this brotherly love is as essential to true Christianity as is the resurrection. It is the proof of discipleship. It is an essential part of one's love for God. It is the required response one must give to all those in the family of God. It is necessary if one is ever to experience heaven.

Koinonia

Endnotes

[1] I Peter 1:22.
[2] John 13:34-35.
[3] Ephesians 2:14-16.
[4] A song often sung by students at Abilene Christian University.
[5] Erick Fromm, *The Art of Loving* (New York: Bantam Books, 1963), p. 15.
[6] See pages 8-10.
[7] Acts 2:44.
[8] Acts 4:32.
[9] II Corinthians 9:13.
[10] II Corinthians 8:24.
[11] I John 3:16-17.
[12] Philippians 4:15.
[13] Philippians 4:18.
[14] I Peter 2:17.
[15] Matthew 22:39; See also Leviticus 19:18.
[16] Luke 10:30-37.
[17] Matthew 5:43.
[18] I John 3:16.
[19] I John 4:9, 11.
[20] I John 4:20-21.
[21] John 13:34; 15:12; I John 3:16.
[22] Romans 5:6-10.
[23] Matthew 25:41-46.
[24] Luke 15:11-32.
[25] Romans 12:10.
[26] Hebrews 13:1-3.

Study Questions

1. Discuss the relationship of love to fellowship.

2. Discuss the relationship of giving and receiving in the practice of love and fellowship.

3. Discuss the importance of brotherly love in the Christian family.

4. Is it true that "love is the symbol by which the world is able to recognize the disciples of Christ?" Discuss.

5. Discuss how fellowship in Christ can be the answer for people trying to escape the things of this world.

6. Fellowship involves a giving and receiving. Discuss these concepts.

7. Discuss the neglect of brotherly love from the story of the prodigal son.

Section 4
Fellowship and Discipline

There is a very close connection between fellowship in Christ and discipline in the church. This is true for at least three reasons.

First, discipline is merely an expression of fellowship. Those who have fellowship in Christ care enough to correct their brethren. Discipline is the flip side of brotherly love.

Second, discipline can only be effective when real fellowship in Christ exists. Discipline accomplishes its purposes only when the fellowship of the church is strong. Discipline can be a shameful farce when the fellowship of the church is weak and/or corrupted.

Third, withdrawal of fellowship is one of the most powerful tools used for discipline in the church. To one who loves the fellowship in Christ, such an action can break a proud and impenitent heart.

Discipline has been sorely neglected in the church in the twentieth century. Such neglect caused Ed Smithson to entitle his book on church discipline, *The Forgotten Commandment*.[1] In some places church discipline has been abused. The giving or withdrawal of fellowship has been used by arrogant leaders to promote their party and club down opposition. Perhaps this abuse has led some to neglect it. In the last few years there have been a number of examples of church discipline leading to litigation. The one being disciplined has sued the church and taken the issue before the courts.[2] Fear of legal action is often the excuse and sometimes the reason given for the neglect of discipline.

There is a need to restore discipline to the fellowship of the church as it was practiced in the New Testament church. Fellowship in Christ is not complete when discipline is neglected. Discipline is not effective without a strong fellowship in Christ. They stand together. Neither is complete without the other.

The church is not a place where "every man does what is right in his own eyes". It is rather a place where each one yields his own will to the will of God and his own preference to that of his brethren. Two things limit a Christian's freedom: first, there is the will of God; second, there is the preference of brethren.

If a brother, in arrogance and selfish pride, rebels against God and the brethren, fellowship is threatened. It is then that discipline must be practiced.

Endnotes

[1] Ed Smithson, *The Forgotten Commandment* (Moore, Oklahoma: Ed Smithson, 1965).
[2] A number of such cases has been reported since 1980. During this time there were highly publicized suits involving churches in Oklahoma, Arkansas and California. A number of these suits are documented and discussed in a series of lectures by Harold Bigham at the Great Commission School, 2093 Wingate Ave., Nashville, Tennessee. The tapes cost $6.00. See also reports in the *Christian Chronicle* 45:6, "Lawsuit: Court Rules for Arkansas Elders", (June, 1988), pages 1, 7 and 45:1, "News Briefs: Collinville Suit Pending", (January, 1988), page 3.

11 / The Needs and Motives of Discipline

"It is not a question of whether God's grace is sufficient, but a question of whether or not a man will repent."

"One of the most unloving acts that one could do — is nothing — when he knows that a brother is being overcome by sin."

It has already been shown that man needs fellowship to overcome his loneliness.[1] It is one of the basic needs of man to live in a community. It takes discipline, however, to hold this community together. Chaos reigns where there is no discipline. A claim to be free becomes a farce when it infringes on the freedom of others. Liberty without discipline becomes license and allows a man to do anything he wants to. This false liberty becomes a flagrant disregard of the rights of others in the community. If there is no discipline, there is no order. Every man becomes a law unto himself. This principle is true in government, in business, in the family and in the church.

Discipline is essential for maturity. The Scriptures outline this principle in discussing how God uses suffering to mature a man. In the context of explaining why the Heavenly Father would allow Christians to suffer, the Scriptures say:

It is for discipline that you endure; God deals with you
as with sons; for what son is there whom his father
does not discipline? But if you are without discipline,
of which all have become partakers, then you are
illegitimate children and not sons. Furthermore, we had
earthly fathers to discipline us, and we respected them;
shall we not much rather be subject to the Father of
spirits, and live? ...All discipline for the moment
seems not to be joyful, but sorrowful; yet to those who
have been trained by it, afterwards it yields the peaceable
fruit of righteousness.[2]

A Christian without discipline is like a spoiled child. A church which does not
use discipline is immature.

A Permissive Society

The western world has been dominated by permissiveness for the last
three decades.

Sexual permissiveness is reflected in the media, art, music and literature.
The majority of the people one meets on the street either reject or ignore all
Scriptural teachings and moral restraints on sexual conduct. Moral permissiveness is reflected in disobedience to law, dishonesty in business and abuse
of the weak. Situational ethics rules the day.

Legal permissiveness is reflected in the liberal legislation and decisions
of the court which favor the criminal more than the victim. Not all things that
are lawful are right — and the people seem to want it so.

The present permissiveness did not come out of a vacuum. Generations
of gradual progression are behind it. Erroneous philosophies have led western
society to accept a continuing erosion of the worth and responsibility of man.

Anthropology is dominated by thought that sees man as a slave to forces
outside himself. John Dewey made man nothing more than the product of his
genes and environment. Calvinism made man nothing more than a puppet of
God — saved or damned according to his predestinated destiny. Sigmund
Freud made man nothing more than a slave to the sexual frustrations harbored
in the deep, dark recesses of the mind. Marx made man nothing more than a
cog in the economic machine of progressive history. Other thinkers have contributed to the current perception that man cannot control his fate or change
his life. The result is a "cop-out culture."

There is change in the wind. Traditional views of man's inability to change or accept responsibility for his conduct are giving way to demands for responsible action and a disciplined life.

The permissive child psychology which once was so popular has been relegated to the archives of a past age of ignorance. A new breed of psychologists are writing about the importance of responsible conduct and about the necessity of discipline. Among the leaders of this latter group are James Dobson with his books, *Dare to Discipline* and *Love Must be Tough* .[3] William Glasser's book *Reality Therapy*, published in 1965, calls for bringing responsibility back to education.[4] Phyllis and David York's works on *Toughlove* seeks to use discipline to change the destructive lifesytle of those involved in the drug culture.[5]

A large group in government is calling for financial responsibility in spending. Courts are more and more demanding a legal responsibility for conduct. Society has grown tired of permissive lawlessness and is calling for law and order.

After a period of sexual permissiveness that seems to rival that of ancient Corinth, there is a renewed call for sexual discipline. This has not come about because of respect for the will of God so much as from the knowledge of the fact that it just will not work. Venereal disease, AIDS and the breakdown of family relationships are but a few of the results of such permissiveness.

People are seeing that they have been "had" by false teachers and unworthy leaders who smooth talked them into believing that "freedom was free" and love is "not having to say you are sorry." People are picking up their broken lives and confessing that they have been deceived. They have discovered the hard way that one cannot ignore the laws of God without consequences; one cannot have freedom without responsibility; one cannot find happiness in raw materialism.

The pied pipers of humanism led a whole generation down the primrose path of self-centered irresponsibility only to find the emptiness of meaningless despair. They had sought to camouflage their permissiveness under the guise of liberty. They now have been exposed for what they really are — reprobate. Peter described such men who sought to bring a "false freedom" to the church in the first century:

> These are springs without water, and mists driven
> by a storm, for whom the black darkness has been
> reserved. For speaking out arrogant words of vanity
> they entice by fleshly desires, by sensuality, those

who barely escape from the ones who live in error,
promising them freedom while they themselves are
slaves of corruption; for by what a man is overcome,
by this he is enslaved.[6]

Love has been redefined by these advocates of false liberty to fit their own ends. For them love centers around self-love. They fail to realize that "doing your own thing" without regard for the feelings or freedom of others is a false love.

Love is longsuffering and forgiving but not permissive. To tolerate sin without reproof is a false love. To be silent when error is advocated is a false love. To be passive in the midst of evil is a false love.

Wrong Motives

One of the greatest reasons for the neglect of church discipline in the fellowship of the church has been its abuse. Wrong motives, wrong methods and wrong reasons for church discipline have been witnessed in enough places and at enough times that the whole practice has been called in question. Memories of ecclesiastical trials, hypocritical self-righteous condemnations, political power struggles and the party spirit all come to mind at the mention of church discipline. When God's plan is abused and made into a perversion, people will be confused and neglect the truth. It appears the devil is able to do more harm by counterfeiting the truth than by advocating blatant error.

One wrong motive for discipline is hypocrisy. In most cases of church discipline the issue of hypocrisy is raised. How can one sinner judge another sinner? How can one cast another to Satan when he is having problems with sin in his own life?

Those who are trying to discipline a brother in sin are judged as being hypocrites. They are accused of exposing the sins of others so their own sins will not look so bad.

Sometimes the charge of hypocrisy is true. Jesus condemned those who demanded of others what they refused to do themselves. Just as Jesus rebuked the hypocrisy of the scribes and Pharisees, so should there be rebuke for those who seek to discipline others while tolerating sin in their own lives.

"The scribes and the Pharisees have seated themselves
in the chair of Moses; therefore all that they tell
you, do and observe, but do not do according to their

deeds; for they say things, and do not do them." And
they tie up heavy loads, and lay them on men's shoulders;
but they themselves are unwilling to move them with
so much as a finger.[7]

There can be no "holier than thou" attitude in true church discipline. It is one brother saved by the grace of God who, with humility, is trying to save another brother who is in the process of being lost through the deceit of the Devil. There can be no self-righteous pride in administering discipline if one heeds the admonition of Paul:

Brethren, even if a man is caught in any trespass,
you who are spiritual, restore such a one in a spirit
of gentleness; looking to yourself, lest you too
be tempted.[8]

Sometimes the charge of hypocrisy is not true. The charge is made in response to loving discipline. The cry of "hypocrisy" is merely a way for the one who has been caught in the wrong to divert attention from his own sin. When one confronts a brother and exposes his sin, one of two responses is expected. Either he will be sorry for his sin and repent or he will harden his heart in rebellion and respond with a charge of "hypocrisy."

When Jesus exposed the sins of the Pharisees, they immediately began picking at him for eating with unwashed hands and plucking grain on the Sabbath. The attempt to intimidate Jesus did not work. He continued to confront their rebellion against God.

Closely connected with the charge of hypocrisy is another charge. It is claimed that exercising discipline makes one Christian judge another. This, they claim, limits the grace of God.

Christians are to judge one another. Such is the admonition of Paul in discussing a case of discipline at Corinth:

Do you not judge those who are within the church? But
those who are outside God judges. REMOVE THE WICKED
MAN FROM AMONG YOURSELVES.[9]

One must not be so afraid that he has a beam in his own eye that he refuses to take a mote out of his brother's eye. If one waited for every Christian to be sinless and the church to be without problems before discipline was practiced, such would never happen.

The grace of God has nothing to do with the issue. It is not a question of whether God's grace is sufficient, but a question of whether or not a man will repent.

There is a big difference between a "redeemed sinner who is walking in the light"[10] and "a rebellious sinner who refuses to repent." The former is assured of the blood of Christ cleansing him from sin. The latter is to be warned of the judgment of God and the discipline of the church. It is just as wrong to neglect the judgment of God as it is the grace of God.

A second wrong motive for church discipline is "politics." Parties in the church sometimes struggle for power. To put down resistance, they "disfellowship" all who oppose them. They "disfellowship" people they do not even know. They "disfellowship" whole congregations because of their connection with someone in the party they oppose. Such is not the practice of New Testament discipline. It is party politics.

Such conduct was known even in the early church. Fellowship then as now was used as an ecclesiastical club to dispose of the opposition. It is condemned:

> I wrote something to the church; but Diotrephes, who
> loves to be first among them, does not accept what we
> say. For this reason, if I come, I will call attention to
> his deeds which he does, unjustly accusing us with
> wicked words; and not satisfied with this, neither
> does he himself receive the brethren, and he forbids
> those who desire to do so, and puts them out of the
> church.[11]

It is a shameful situation when leaders in the church try to line Christians up into warring parties. In their desire for power they try to force all the members of the church to "take their stand" on one side or the other. They try to crystallize these parties through yellow journalism, fear tactics and disfellowshipping. No doctrine or moral issues are involved — just leaders with a "Diotrephes syndrome" trying to maintain control.

There are hundreds of churches who are still suffering from the shame of the "Diotrephes" of the past who split churches for nothing more than getting their own way. It is ridiculous to see several churches in the same small town, suspicious of one another, but teaching the same Gospel. People who cause and promote such suspicion and division are condemned for practicing all seven of the things that the Lord hates:

There are six things which the Lord hates, Yes, seven
which are an abomination to Him: Haughty eyes, a
lying tongue, And hands that shed innocent blood, A
heart that devises wicked plans, Feet that run rapidly
to evil, A false witness who utters lies, And one who
spreads strife among brothers.[12]

One of the consequences of this abuse of church discipline is that good and
godly men become afraid to follow the Scriptural way. What must be realized
is this: the same thing will occur whether or not church discipline is practiced.
False teachers and divisive party leaders arise in every generation. More and
better unity can be maintained if the Scriptural pattern of church discipline is
followed. There would never have been a Diotrephes church boss if he had
been disciplined by the brethren instead of tolerating his "takeover."

A third wrong motive for church discipline is retaliation. It is not the
Christian way to respond to those who hurt you by returning the hurt. Jesus
teaches "turning the other cheek" and "going the second mile." When a
brother has shamed the church by his conduct or dragged the name of
"Christian" through the gutter, the devil tempts one to "get even." "Eye for eye
and tooth for tooth" seems to be the way to respond. Not so! There is no
retaliation in church discipline. The Christian way is to "not be overcome by
evil, but to overcome evil with good."[13] Strong discipline in the spirit of
brotherhood is the teaching of Paul:

And if anyone does not obey our instruction in
this letter, take special note of that man and do not
associate with him, so that he may be put to shame.
And yet do not regard him as an enemy, but admonish
him as a brother.[14]

It is a desire for repentance, not retaliation, that is the motive for true church
discipline.

It is easy to see the temptation to discipline for retaliation. Someone hurts
the church. He shames the church. Members of the church are embarrassed
and hurt. The name of Jesus has been shamed. The blood of Jesus has been
trodden under foot. The brother ought to know better. Why would he do such
a thing? People outside the church know about it, and this influences their
attitude toward all members of the church.

After the first wave of pain and shame passes, a spirit of anger rises within the heart. One hates the sin and soon he starts hating the sinner. He wants to dissociate himself from the shame. He wants to forget the pain. He wants to "get even" with the one who caused it. There is a temptation to close the eyes and harden the heart and "church him."

This kind of retaliative discipine does not work. It will not restore the sinner nor will it do any good for the church. Most people are able to see through the veneer of pretended holiness and know that what happened was really a reaction to one's own frustration.

The first concern of discipline is the restoration of the sinner. This restoration sometimes demands that we absorb the shame which his sin has brought on the church. This restoration sometimes means "undeserved forgiveness" for his wrongdoing. After all, this is the kind of forgiveness that God gives to every sinner who turns from his sins in repentance. Such response is taught by Paul:

> Bearing with one another, and forgiving each other,
> whoever has a complaint against any one; just as the
> Lord forgave you, so also should you.[15]

The Christian's prayer for a brother who has sinned against God and the church should be the same as Jesus' prayer on the cross: "Father forgive them; for they do not know what they are doing."[16]

Right Motives

The right motive[17] for discipline is brotherly love. Discipline is ineffective without brotherly love. Brotherly love is incomplete without discipline. They go together like faith and obedience. Discipline can be called the flip side of love.

Love has two sides. One side is positive. It involves acceptance, forgiveness, self-sacrifice and giving. The other side is more negative. It involves confrontation, reproof and discipline. To neglect the positive side makes love cold and selfish. To neglect the negative side makes love shallow and selfish. Either extreme is a false love.

The flip side of love is often neglected. It is "tough love." It is sometimes threatening, hard and negative. It is not easy for either the giver or the receiver. It involves a lover confronting his loved one to bring about needed change. It is the strongest kind of love. It cares enough to correct. It is the highest kind of love because it requires the greatest risk.

The father disciplining his child is taking the risk of rejection in order to make his child better. The husband or wife confronting his or her spouse's misconduct is taking the risk of rejection in order to correct the wrong. The teacher correcting an irresponsible student is taking the risk of rejection to make him into a better person. The teen-ager confronting a friend because of unacceptable conduct is taking the risk of rejection by forcing him to see the need for change. The church confronting one of its members who is continuing in sin is taking the risk of rejection in order to save his soul.

It is indeed a weak love relationship which will not risk a friendship to save his brother's soul from hell. If it be necessary to affirm truth in order to correct an error believed by a brother, so be it. One may risk a friendship, but it is more essential to attempt to save a soul. Paul faced this dilemma when correcting the error of the brethren in Galatia. He asked them a rhetorical question:

> Have I therefore become your enemy by telling you
> the truth?[18]

It is not love which causes one to refuse to confront a brother who is involved in sin for fear of losing a friend. It is just the opposite. That "ooey-gooey," "wishy-washy," compromising sentimentality which refuses to confront error, oppose sin and speak out against evil is as far away from brotherly love as day is from night.

True brotherly love cares enough to try and keep a brother from acting like a fool. It tells him when he is wrong even though he might not like it at the time. It tries to keep him from hurting himself and others by his wrongdoing. It risks a relationship on earth in order to try and save his soul for heaven. This is the kind of love which motivates one to follow the instructions of Jude:

> ...save others, snatching them out of the fire; and
> on some have mercy with fear, hating even the garment
> polluted by the flesh.[19]

An Old Testament proverb expresses the necessity of discipline in a love relationship:

My son, do not reject the discipline of the Lord, Or loathe
His reproof, For whom the Lord loves He reproves, Even
as a father, the son in whom he delights.[20]

Twice this proverb is alluded to in the New Testament to show the connection
of love and discipline:

FOR THOSE WHOM THE LORD LOVES HE DISCIPLINES,
AND HE SCOURGES EVERY SON WHOM HE RECEIVES.[21]

Those whom I love, I reprove and discipline; be
zealous therefore and repent.[22]

The first passage is in the context of a Christian accepting trials as being God-
given discipline to make him better. The second passage is a statement of Jesus
to the church at Laodicea. He warns them that without repentance, the "love
of God" would cause them to be "spit out" of the Lord's mouth.

Discipline is not an ecclesiastical club to punish the weak sheep, but it is
a shepherd's staff to save the lost and protect the innocent. If the shepherd's
staff is used to protect the sheep, the devouring wolf might view the staff as a
club—and such it is to him. If the shepherd's staff is used to bring a sheep back
into the fold, the wayward sheep might view the staff as a chastening rod —
and such it might be to him. Discipline, like a shepherd's staff, can be
interpreted different ways. Whether it is a chastening rod of love or a club of
vengeance is determined by both the way it is received and the motives with
which it is administered.

The tough side of love is often misunderstood. Perhaps this brief com-
mentary on Paul's description of love will bring this neglected side of love into
better focus:

Love is patient — but not permissive.[23]

Love is kind enough to try to correct sin in another —
even if it means making him an enemy.[24]

Love is not jealous of another's worth — but neither does he
demean his own worth by refusing to confront sin and error
that is leveled against him.[25]

Love does not brag — but neither does it remain silent
when that of which one is a part comes under reproach.[26]

Love is not arrogant — but neither does it let abusive,
dishonest charges go unchallenged.[27]

Love does not act unbecomingly — but it does act. The
most unloving act possible is to do nothing when for
the truth one ought to die.[28]

Love does not seek its own power and glory — if it means
compromising with evil.[29]

Love is not easily provoked — but neither is it passive
to sin.[30]

Love does not take into account a wrong suffered — but
neither does it condone wrong by refusing to
oppose it.[31]

Love does not rejoice in unrighteousness, but it rejoices
in truth — even when that unrighteousness is
practiced by one's family and truth exposes the sins
of one's friends.[32]

Love bears all things — even the rejection of friends
because it cares enough to correct.[33]

Love believes all things — even that a sinner can be
brought to repentance by confrontation.[34]

Love hopes all things — even for repentance in the
heart of the sinner by telling him his sin.[35]

Love endures all things — even the rejection of loved
ones because their wrong is exposed.[36]

Love never fails — even when one's motives for tough
love are misunderstood, criticized and opposed

— even when one must sacrifice approval and
acceptance in order to bring about righteous
change.[37]

The motive for discipline in the church is love. One of the most unloving acts
that one could do — is nothing — when he knows that a brother is being
overcome by sin.

Observations

There is too little moral and ethical difference between the church and the
world. Just as Corinth was rebuked because it tolerated "immorality of such
kind as does not exist among the Gentiles,"[38] so the twentieth century church
sometimes tolerates immorality such as does not even exist in denominations.
Undisciplined immorality in the church nullifies the "proof of claim" of being
the New Testament church just as much as instrumental music and sprinkling
for baptism.

Unless there is a restoration of church discipline, there will be an apostasy
of a large segment of the church. It is true that the church seems to be in a
constant state of apostasy and restoration in every generation. Some fell away
when the charismatic movement swept the nation. Some fell away into
theological liberalism and open fellowship. These are only very minor aposta-
sies in comparison to what is going to happen if churches do not start teaching
and practicing church discipline.

Unless there is a restoration of the New Testament pattern of church
discipline, there will be a continued decline in evangelism and church growth
in coming years. A major reason for the decline in evangelism is permissiveness in the church. That which allows anything, means nothing. All of the
pumped up programs of evangelism and new techniques of church growth
mean nothing if churches of Christ do not maintain a doctrinal and moral
distinctiveness. If the church does not have a distinctive faith, a distinctive
message and a distinctive life-style, it has nothing to say. If one does not have
a faith for which to contend, there is no basis for evangelism.

Like Corinth of old, some have become "arrogant" and are proud of their
permissiveness:

It is actually reported that there is immorality
among you, and immorality of such a kind as does

not exist even among the Gentiles ...And you have
become arrogant, and have not mourned instead.[39]

Some churches, like Corinth, delight in the fact that their fellowship is liberal
enough to tolerate impenitent adulterers, known false teachers, habitual
drunkards and practicing swindlers.

Like Thyatira of old, some churches tolerate false teachers and immorality without resistance — or even concern. Jesus condemned such:

But I have this against you, that you tolerate the
woman Jezebel, who calls herself a prophetess, and she
teaches and leads My bondservants astray, so that they
commit acts of immorality and eat things sacrificed
to idols.[40]

It was wrong for Jezebel to teach error and lead Christians into immorality. It
was just as wrong for the church to tolerate it. In tolerating it, they became a
partaker in her sin.

Too many twentieth century churches are fast approaching a crisis
climate in regard to church discipline. If the New Testament pattern is not
restored soon, they will be on the downhill slide into apostasy.

It is tragic to see an undisciplined family in which the children are spoiled
and the adolescents rebel. Such a family is miserable in their relationships and
doomed to disintegration. Family fellowship was lost because true love was
not practiced.

The same tragedy happens in a church when discipline is neglected. This
accounts for bad church relationships and will finally result in the demise of
the church. Fellowship and discipline go together.

Endnotes

[1]See pages 121-123.
[2]Hebrews 12:7-9, 11.
[3]James Dobson, *Love Must Be Tough* , (Waco: Word Books, 1983).
[4]William Glasser, *Reality Therapy* , (New York: Harper and Row, 1965).
[5]Phyllis and David York, *Toughlove, A Self Help Manual For Kids in Trouble* ,
(Sellersville, Pennsylvania: Community Service Foundation, 1983).
[6]II Peter 2:17-19.

[7]Matthew 23:2-4.
[8]Galatians 6:1.
[9]I Corinthians 5:12-13.
[10]I John 1:7-9.
[11]III John 9-10.
[12]Proverbs 6:16-19.
[13]Romans 12:21.
[14]II Thessalonians 3:14-15.
[15]Colossians 3:13.
[16]Luke 23:34.
[17]The author makes a distinction between the motives and the purposes of discipline in the fellowship of the church. This chapter deals with the motives for discipline. Chapter 13 will deal with the purposes of discipline.
[18]Galatians 4:16.
[19]Jude 23.
[20]Proverbs 3:11-12.
[21]Hebrews 12:6.
[22]Revelation 3:19.
[23]John 8:11. The woman taken in adultery was told to "go your way; from now on sin no more."
[24]Galatians 4:16.
[25]Confronting abusive conduct must conform to the principle of "turning the other cheek," but it also must conform to pronouncing the judgment of God upon evil and error. See Jude 9.
[26]Jesus showed that His conduct of eating with tax collectors and sinners was more in conformity with the Scriptures than that of the scribes and Pharisees. See Matthew 9:10-13.
[27]Jesus confronted the false charges of the Pharisees and exposed their inconsistency. See Matthew 12:24-28.
[28]When Peter was told by the council not to speak any more in the name of Jesus, he refused to obey and acted with zealous faith. See Acts 4:19-20.
[29]Jesus refused to cater to the whims of the multitude even if it meant that His disciples would grumble and many would turn back from following Him. See John 6:60-66.
[30]See John 2:15.
[31]See I Corinthians 5:1-2.
[32]See Matthew 23:37-38.
[33]See Galatians 4:16.
[34]See Matthew 3:11.

[35]See Matthew 18:15.
[36]See Hebrews 12:6.
[37]Paul dealt with false teachers at Corinth who tried to undermine his relationship with the church by false charges, criticism and ridicule. See II Corinthians 11.
[38]I Corinthians 5:1.
[39]I Corinthians 5:1-2.
[40]Revelation 2:20.

Study Questions

1. Why is there a need for the practice of church discipline?

2. In practicing discipline, what motives are important?

3. Can you give examples (biblical, and otherwise) where motives have not been right for the practice of discipline?

4. How do you relate love to the practice of discipline?

5. How does fellowship relate to the practice of church discipline?

6. Why is discipline essential for maturity?

7. How does man's inability to accept responsibility for his conduct effect a disciplined life?

8. Discuss the difference between "a redeemed sinner who is walking in the light" and " a rebellious sinner who refuses to repent."

Koinonia

12 / The Process of Discipline

> *"If the church of Jesus Christ is restored in the twentieth century, it will be found practicing discipline..."*
>
> *"A brother who refuses to repent of sin will not hesitate to lie to justify his actions."*

Fellowship Support

The process of continual self renewal in the church does not begin with discipline. Discipline is only one of many means that the church has for "building up of itself in love."[1] It has been said, "to cut off an offender is good, to cure him is better, but to prevent him from falling is best of all."

Fellowship in Christ is established by the new birth into the family of God. It is sealed with the Holy Spirit of promise. It is exercised in caring for one another, sharing with one another and bearing one another's burdens. It is bound together in brotherly love.

The body of Christ, the church, renews itself much as the physical body renews itself. Wounds are healed and sickness is cured by the interaction of different members of the physical body. There is constant renewal through the intake of nourishment and the throwing off of waste. Without this renewal the

Koinonia

physical body would die. Without a constant spiritual renewal of the body of Christ, the church will also die.

It has already been shown that in the process of self renewal the church is involved in correcting and strengthening its different members.[2]

> The ignorant are taught.
> The depressed are encouraged.
> The neglectful are reproved.
> The rebellious are rebuked.
> The unruly are admonished.
> The impenitent are cast to Satan.
> Prayers are given for all.

Just as the physical body seeks to maintain the health of all of its members, so also does the body of Christ. This is accomplished only when there is a healthy fellowship.

Levels of Fellowship

A Christian lives in a world where he is involved in different levels and varied kinds of fellowship. These various fellowships are based on different kinds of relationships and involve different kinds of responsibilities. Most of them do not include the spiritual fellowship which is known in Christ.

Level #1 is a fellowship involving all of mankind.[3] Men are "brothers" in Adam who are alien from one another in life. A Christian's fellowship responsibilities go beyond the fellowship he has in Christ. He also has a responsibility to his neighbor. Loving one's neighbor is the second commandment of Jesus.[4] Jesus illustrated this command by giving the parable of the good Samaritan.[5] Being a neighbor involves sharing, caring, and bearing the burdens for any man — even a total stranger. There is a fellowship involving all of humanity.

Level #2 is a fellowship involving those of common ethnic origin. Peter called Jews "brethren" when he addressed them on the day of Pentecost before any of them were in the family of God.[6] Ananias called Saul of Tarsus "brother" before he became a Christian.[7] Paul called the Jewish mob "brethren" even though they were opposed to Jesus Christ. There is a fellowship involving national origin.

Level #3 is a fellowship involving family. It is possible to have a fellowship with those in the family circle without having a spiritual fellowship with them in Jesus Christ. The wife who has an unbelieving husband is told to submit to him.[8] She has a family fellowship with him even though he is not a Christian. Such a family fellowship is of God. It must not be broken by the Christian just because he is an unbeliever.

> And a woman who has an unbelieving husband, and he
> consents to live with her, let her not send her
> husband away.[9]

There is a binding household fellowship sanctioned by God because it is based on the family relationship.

Level #4 is a fellowship involving community. One lives in the world and must relate to the people of the world. Hardly a day goes by that one is not called on to have a social relationship, a business relationship or a civic relationship with those who are not in the family of God. Paul recognized this reality:

> I wrote you in my letter not to associate with immoral
> people; I did not at all mean with the immoral people
> of this world, or with the covetous and swindlers, or
> with idolaters; for then you would have to go out of
> the world.[10]

Though Paul recognizes the validity of certain contact with the unbelieving community, he emphasizes that one must not allow this to compromise one's faith. The fellowship involved in community must not come in conflict with the fellowship involved in Christ:

> Do not be bound together with unbelievers; for
> what partnership have righteousness and lawlessness,
> or what fellowship has light with darkness? Or what
> harmony has Christ with Belial, or what has a believer
> in common with an unbeliever?[11]

Fellowship in community is not on the same level as the unique fellowship in Christ. Fellowship in Christ is a spiritual fellowship. It is stronger than and has priority over any other relationship in the world.

Level # 5 is a fellowship involving all of God's children. It is a spiritual fellowship and therefore finds its basis in a different sphere of existence. It involves all of those who have experienced the new birth in baptism. They are brothers by birth. Once they are born of God, they are His children and a brother to all children of God. It is impossible to "unbrother" them no matter what they do or say.

This does not mean that they will remain in fellowship with God. It does not mean that the church will always extend fellowship to them. They might become prodigal sons who leave the Father's house. They might become sons who refused to follow the instructions of the Father, and the church must remain aloof from them.[12] They might become brothers who have been cast to Satan and cut off from the fellowship of the church.[13] They remain brothers though not in fellowship with God's family.

Different phrases are used to refer to this break in fellowship in God's family. Some seem more severe than others. Those involved in the break in fellowship represent different kinds of people involved in different kinds of sins. This may infer that there is not just one rule or method which must be applied to every circumstance. Note the differences:

> Christians are to *keep aloof from* those who refused
> to follow the traditions received from Paul.[14]

> Disciples of Christ were to *regard* brethren who refused
> the discipline of the church *as Gentiles and tax-gatherers*.[15]

> Brethren were to *keep your eyes on* and *turn away from*
> those who were causing dissensions at Rome.[16]

> The church is told not *to receive ...into your house*
> or even *give greetings* to those who do not abide in
> the teaching of Christ.[17]

> Saints at Corinth were instructed to *deliver to Satan* and
> *not even to eat* with an impenitent immoral brother.[18]

Fellowship was broken in each case, but it would appear that the action taken was in keeping with the severity of the sin. Christians at Thessalonica were to keep aloof from those who were neglectful of following the instructions of Paul, but one was not even to eat with the impenitent immoral brother at

Corinth. Could it be that the medicine of discipline is to be administered according to the severity of the spiritual sickness?

There appears to be a distinction made between how one should deal with a perverted "factious man" and a brother who "sins against you."[19] Three steps are involved in correcting a brother who "sins against you" before he is to be regarded as a "Gentile and a tax-gatherer." Only two warnings are to be given to a "factious man" before he is rejected.

> Reject a factious man after a first and second warning,
> knowing that such a man is perverted and is sinning,
> being self-condemned.[20]

Is it possible that the process of dealing with a factious false teacher in Crete was more severe because of the danger which would be involved by "telling it to the church"? One would not want to give an open forum to a false teacher.

Other passages reflecting the practice of discipline in the early church pose difficult questions. These questions cause one to be careful about putting down rules and regulations beyond what is written in the Scriptures.

What does the "right hand of fellowship" mean? Paul and Barnabas received such:

> ...James and Cephas and John, who were reputed
> to be pillars, gave to me and Barnabas the right hand
> of fellowship, that we might go to the Gentiles, and
> they to the circumcised.[21]

Were Paul and Barnabas in any kind of fellowship with the brethren at Jerusalem before they received this? It would appear so. At least Luke said Peter called them "brethren."[22] If they were in fellowship, what did "receiving the right hand of fellowship" imply? The context seems to indicate that Peter, James and John gave sanction to the Gospel message preached by Paul and Barnabas. When one's teachings were approved they received the "right hand of fellowship." When they were not approved, they were denied hospitality.[23]

What was the fellowship relationship between Paul and Barnabas after they broke up over taking John Mark on their second journey? Their disagreement was so great that they refused to travel together:

> And after some days Paul said to Barnabas, "Let us
> return and visit the brethren in every city in which we

proclaimed the word of the Lord, and see how they are."
And Barnabas was desirous of taking John, called Mark,
along with them also. But Paul kept insisting that they
should not take him along who had deserted them in
Pamphylia and had not gone with them to the work.
And there arose such a sharp disagreement that they
separated from one another.[24]

In spite of this disagreement, Paul could later speak of him in terms of approval.[25] Is it possible for brothers to be in a heated personal disagreement over non-essential matters and still know a deep spiritual fellowship with one another? The example of Paul and Barnabas seems to suggest that it is. It should be noted that their disagreement was not over an issue upon which God had spoken. It was over a personal opinion concerning the qualifications of a traveling companion. If God had spoken on the issue, it would no longer have been an opinion; it would have been a Divine teaching — a doctrine.[26]

It soon becomes evident that the only way to understand the exact meaning of "fellowship" in any passage of Scripture is to define it in the context in which it is used. It is folly to use — in an uncritical way — an admonition about fellowship in one text with the meaning of fellowship in another text.

Sometimes fellowship is limited. There is a civil fellowship that is not a spiritual fellowship. In this world one is constantly sharing with others in social, business and domestic relationships. Such relationships are "limited fellowships" and are not as great as "full fellowship" in Christ. Fellowship does not mean that one always approves of everything that is done by the one with whom he is sharing. It does not always mean endorsement or approval.

Sometimes fellowship involves sanction. This seemed to be the meaning of what is called the "right hand of fellowship" in Galatians 2:9. This also seems to be the meaning in II John 11. Hospitality was to be denied to false teachers because "the one who gives him greeting participates in his evil deeds."[27] The same meaning is reflected in Paul's teachings against idolatry. Christians taking part in sacrificing to idols were corrected because "I do not want you to become sharers in demons."[28]

Leaving the Fellowship

The process of discipline in the church presupposes that the one who is being disciplined is "in fellowship." If they were not, then such action would be empty and ineffective. Discipline involves the possibility of "withdrawing fellowship." One cannot withdraw that which is not there. It is because of the failure to recognize this fundamental fact that so often church discipline seems to be a failure.

The one who was disciplined does not repent. The discipline was too little and too late. He had already disconnected himself from the fellowship of the church so there was no motivation for repentance in "withdrawing fellowship." If the church seeks to withdraw that which does not exist, it is no more than an exercise in futility. It is a meaningless, useless activity. Alexander Campbell made such a judgment in *The Christian System:*

> A person can not be under the oversight or under the
> discipline of a congregation, unless he voluntarily
> associates with the brethren meeting in that place,
> and unless it be a matter of notoriety or of record
> among the brethren that he is one of them. There can
> be no formal exclusion if there be no formal reception.[29]

The father of the prodigal son did not withdraw fellowship from his child when he left home. Fellowship was broken by the action of his son. The father was passive in the broken relationship. He only suffered from the pain inflicted by his wayward son. The choice of the broken relationship was that of the selfish son.

John records how some left the fellowship of the church on their own initiative.

> They went out from us, but they were not really of us;
> for if they had been of us, they would have remained
> with us; but they went out, in order that it might be
> shown that they all are not of us.[30]

This passage shows that fellowship was broken, not by John or the church, but by those who left the fellowship. They were mavericks, not wanting to be fenced in by the teachings of Christ. There was no possibility for John or the church to exercise discipline on them. There was no fellowship to be withdrawn. There were no ties by which they could be recalled. They had been broken. The only thing to do was what John did. He recognized that the fellowship was broken by the maverick brethren. This let the rest of the brethren know they were not in the fellowship with Christ and were not to be received by members of the church.

There should be a distinction between "withdrawing fellowship" and a recognition that "no fellowship exists." If a brother by his own decision and announcement "quits the church," he is not in fellowship. If a brother by his long-time practice has willfully isolated himself from the fellowship of the church, he is not in fellowship—by definition. Withdrawing fellowship is impossible. There is none to take away. The only thing that can be done is to recognize the condition. The brother has withdrawn himself, and the church acknowledges it.

These passages instruct the contemporary church. One cannot withdraw fellowship which is not there. It is foolish for brethren to think that they can "clean up" an old church membership roll by writing "withdrawal letters" to all who have not attended the assemblies for a certain number of times during the past year. The folly is in the non-Biblical and non-personal way that it is done. The folly is in the neglect of fellowship that led to those brethren not being in the assemblies. The folly is in the fact that there exists no fellowship to be withdrawn.

This is not to say that such delinquent Christians are to be ignored. No! A thousand times, No! Seek to restore fellowship by caring, sharing, and bearing with the burdens of their lives. If fellowship cannot be restored and they continue to refuse the responsibility of fellowship in the church, then the church should recognize what has already happened. They are not in fellowship. They have withdrawn themselves from the fellowship. The church should know about it and be involved—not as a part of a discipline procedure, but as being made aware of the fact that this brother has, on his own initiative, rejected the fellowship in Christ.

Steps of Discipline

There are a number of examples of discipline being practiced in the early church,[31] but most of them do not outline a clear pattern on how it was done. Apostolic authority is often involved. The secret sin of Ananias and Sapphira was revealed to Peter by inspiration. The process of their discipline also came through inspiration.[32] Apostolic authority was involved in the instructions on how to discipline the immoral brother in the church at Corinth, the false teacher at Ephesus, and the unruly at Thessalonica.[33] Evangelistic responsibility is involved in reproving a sinner and admonishing a factious man.[34]

Discipline in the church today cannot be directed by inspiration or personal apostolic authority. Evangelistic responsibility involves reproving and admonishing, but there is no authority for imposing discipline. Some factors of human judgment must be used to determine the process.[35]

There is help to be found in the teachings of Jesus. Jesus Himself instructs how one is to deal with a brother who sins against another brother. Distinctive steps are to be followed. It is first to be dealt with as a personal matter between the two. If it cannot be resolved this way, then it becomes a "church matter." When it becomes a "church matter," Jesus tells how it is to be done. The process is clear. When this practice is rejected, it is not done so because it is hard to understand — but because it is hard to practice:

> And if your brother sins, go and reprove him in private;
> if he listens to you, you have won your brother. But if
> he does not listen to you, take one or two more with
> you, so that BY THE MOUTH OF TWO OR THREE WITNESSES
> EVERY FACT MAY BE CONFIRMED. And if he refuses to
> listen to them, tell it to the church; and if he refuses
> to listen even to the church, let him be to you as a
> Gentile and a tax-gatherer.[36]

There are four steps given by Jesus. First, there is personal confrontation. Second, there is confirmation before witnesses. Third, there is public concern and contact by the church. Fourth, there is a withdrawal of brotherly fellowship so as to make him as a Gentile.

It would appear that these steps were not followed in all of the examples of discipline in the epistles. Personal apostolic authority, inspiration and evangelistic responsibility are included in these cases. More was involved than an issue between two brothers. Though one must be careful not to bind this "four step" process on every case of discipline, it is a pattern to follow in any case in which there is a sin committed against another brother.

The first step is to "Go and reprove him in private." This is a personal confrontation. It is still a private matter between two brothers. Much is involved in this confrontation. It is not "clubbing him with condemnation" or "belittling him through one's own self-righteous pride." It is tender brotherly correction. Paul describes it thus:

> Brethren, even if a man is caught in any trespass,
> you who are spiritual, restore such a one in a spirit
> of gentleness; looking to yourself, lest you too
> be tempted.[37]

The spirit of gentleness will help open the heart so the correction will be received.

The holy, spiritual life of the corrector will also help the one who is corrected to listen. He will not be guilty of having a log in his own eye while trying to take a speck out of his brother's eye.[38]

Correcting a brother who has sinned and is lost must not be regarded as a matter of convenience. When one knows of a brother's sin, then it becomes his responsibility to seek to correct him. To neglect to do so places one's own soul in jeopardy. Such was the judgment of God against prophets of the Old Testament:

> When I say to the wicked, 'You shall surely die'; and you
> do not warn him or speak out to warn the wicked from his
> wicked way that he may live, that wicked man shall die in
> his iniquity, but his blood I will require at your hand.[39]

What kind of man would neglect to warn a neighbor of the impending danger of a fire? What kind of person would not seek to keep a child from picking up a rattlesnake? What kind of brother would refuse to warn his sister of the danger of taking cocaine? The answer to all of these questions is this: *The same kind of person who would not confront his brother about a soul-damning sin* .

"Go and tell" is the first step. If this step is successful, the issue is dropped. Nothing else needs to be done. The sin is corrected and the fellowship is saved.

The second step is to "take one or two with you." This step is taken only if the first step is rejected. It is to provide confirmation before witnesses. If the sinning brother refuses to heed the private confrontation, witnesses are needed. One or two are enough.

The purpose is to have another's testimony besides one's own of what actually took place. Such is in keeping with the demands of the Old Testament law. The legal language of Deuteronomy 19:15 is quoted. If any public accusation is brought against a man, it must be more than "his word against yours." There must be two or three witnesses. There are two reasons for this.

First, it is to confirm what took place when the sinner was confronted with his sin. What was the accusation? What was the sinner's response? If it is necessary to bring the matter before the church, the testimony of more than one person is needed for confirmation. A brother who refuses to repent of sin will not hesitate to lie to justify his actions. One needs witnesses in talking with such people. The confronted party may lie and bring a false report about what happened in the confrontation.

Second, it is to give greater persuasion in restoring the brother. A brother in sin might reject one brother's admonition. It is not so easy to reject the admonition of two or three. He knows he cannot "weasel out" of his sin. What he says is on record and he cannot deny it later. It becomes more than a private disagreement between two. The pressure to repent increases. All of the love, influence and truth-power of the witnesses are added to that of the brother who first confronted the sinful brother. If this step is successful, the issue is dropped.

If the brother does not repent, the issue is no longer private. He is a member of the church. What affects him affects the body. It is time for all of the loving resources of the church to be brought to bear in order to bring this brother to repentance.

The third step is "tell it to the church." It is a public confrontation of the sinner. All of the influence and power of the total church is focused on bringing this brother to repentance. Never let it be said, "we did everything we could to recall a brother or sister from sin" until this step is taken. Such a statement may serve as an excuse for "washing one's hands of guilt," but it is dishonest.

Many are lost today because the church did not follow this step. Why is there such a hesitancy to "tell it to the church?" Do we not care enough to correct? Do we not trust the brethren? Do we not believe God's plan is effective?

Certainly there is a risk. Some well-meaning brother might confront the sinful brother in a crude way. So be it. If everything else has failed to restore a brother, who is to say that this way is not the best? Sometimes people will spread rumors and cause confusion. Maybe so. Such will not be the case nearly so much when the facts of the case are in the open. Members of the church already know something is wrong. To conceal the facts is foolish. The healthy and scriptural way is to "tell it to the church." One must not fear truth. He who practices truth comes to the light. It is the one who does evil that refuses to come to the light.[40]

When the church is told, false rumors stop. The frustration of caring Christians can now be overcome because they are able to share in the positive response of the whole body. Everyone joins together in a noble act of corrective fellowship to save a sinner.

If such an expression of body life were more often practiced, it would revolutionize the church. The practice of immorality would be curbed. Members of the church would feel closer to one another. Neglectful and erring members would return to the fellowship. Respect for the purity of the church would rise in the community.

The fourth step is "Let him be to you as a Gentile and a tax-gatherer." This involves public rejection by the church. When a brother cannot be restored through the other three steps, then this step is necessary. It must be done for both the good of the sinner and the good of the church.

In tolerating sin, the church allows it to spread. Tolerating sin does not do the sinner any good. It does not do the church any good. It corrupts the holiness of the church.

We have a clear example of this step in the New Testament. Paul's instruction to the church at Corinth was "in the name of our Lord Jesus, when you are assembled ...deliver such a one to Satan."[41] There is no question about what Paul meant in this passage. Six phrases are used to emphasize the point that the sinful brother was to be expelled from the fellowship:

> ...be removed
> ...deliver to Satan
> ...clean out
> ...not to associate
> ...not even to eat with such a one
> ...remove the wicked man

All of the teaching and preaching in the world is not going to be very effective in combating the present flood of immorality in the church until discipline is practiced. It will put teeth into the message. To say one thing and practice another is hypocrisy. Too often members of the church believe the principle of discipline but reject the practice. Faith without works is still dead.

To be regarded as a Gentile and tax-collector does not mean that one is past saving. It just means that the church is not to associate with the excluded brother. The conduct of Gentiles and tax-collectors was obnoxious to Jews. They did not want to associate with them. They were the most repulsive group that a Jew could imagine. To eat with a Gentile was taboo. They were excluded from any fellowship. Such was to be the fate of a disciplined brother.

Examples from the practice of discipline in the epistles confirm this conduct of non-association.

> ...not to associate with him[42]
> ...not to eat a meal or open one's home in hospitality[43]
> ...not bid God's speed[44]
> ...hold yourself aloof from him[45]
> ...have no company with him[46]

Such action is drastic. It is so because there is a crisis. If a brother is on the verge of being lost, drastic action must be taken to save him. To one who loves the church, nothing can be more effective in recalling him from sin than to know that he could suffer loss of fellowship if he refuses to repent.

Practicing church discipline has never been easy. There is the danger of abuse. There is the emotional trauma involved in dealing with brothers and sisters who are deeply loved. There is the risk of rejection. There is the fear of becoming a self-righteous judge or being called a hypocrite. The exercise of church discipline is particularly difficult in the present permissive culture.

Such difficulty must not deter its practice. It is for the good of the church. It is for the good of the one disciplined. It is for the glory of God. If the church of Jesus Christ is restored in the twentieth century, it will be found practicing discipline.

Endnotes

[1]Ephesians 4:16.
[2]See pages 126-129.
[3]The levels of fellowship noted in this section are arbitrarily given for comparison reasons. They are not absolute but intertwine with one another. They may be classified in other ways also.
[4]Matthew 22:39.
[5]Luke 10:30-37.
[6]Acts 2:29.
[7]Acts 9:17.
[8]I Peter 3:1.
[9]I Corinthians 7:13.
[10]I Corinthians 5:9-10.
[11]II Corinthians 6:14-15.
[12]II Thessalonians 3:6, 14-15.
[13]I Timothy 1:20.
[14]II Thessalonians 3:6.
[15]Matthew 18:17.
[16]Romans 16:17.
[17]II John 9-11.
[18]I Corinthians 5:5, 11. See also I Timothy 1:19-20 which also speaks of Hymenaeus being delivered to Satan because of his teaching of faith destroying doctrine.

[19]Matthew 18:15 and Titus 3:10-11.
[20]Titus 3:10-11.
[21]Galatians 2:9.
[22]Acts 15:7.
[23]II John 9-11.
[24]Acts 15:36-39.
[25]See I Corinthians 9:6; Galatians 2:9; Colossians 4:10.
[26]It is uncritical thinking to suggest the disagreement between Paul and Barnabas is an example of dealing with doctrinal differences in the church. As far as it can be determined in the Scriptures, the differences between Paul and Barnabas involved no point of inspired teaching — doctrine. Such is not the case with baptism, the Lord's Supper and worship in song. Substituting infant sprinkling for baptism, adding pizza to the Lord's Supper, and using instrumental music in singing praise are not items of private judgment. They are the innovations of man which "God commanded not." God has spoken about these things and man is not at liberty to change what God has decreed.
[27]*koinonei* is one of the fellowship words and is translated "participate."
[28]I Corinthians 10:20. The word translated "sharers" is *koinonous*.
[29]Alexander Campbell, *The Christian System* (Cincinnati: Standard Publishing Co., 1835), p. 67.
[30]I John 2:19.
[31]There are examples of discipline because of fornication at Corinth, unruliness at Thessalonica, false teachers at Ephesus and schismatics at Rome.
[32]Acts 5:1-11.
[33]I Corinthians 5:3-5; I Timothy 1:20; II Thessalonians 3:6, 14-15.
[34]I Timothy 5:20; Titus 3:10-11.
[35]Richard Norman, *Another Look at Corrective Church Discipline* (Austin: Firm Foundation, 1975), pp. 501, 507. This article shows that there is no "steps" pattern to be found in the examples of discipline in the epistles.
[36]Matthew 18:15-17.
[37]Galatians 6:1.
[38]Matthew 7:1-5.
[39]Ezekiel 3:18.
[40]John 3:20.
[41]I Corinthians 5:4-5.
[42]I Corinthians 5:9.
[43]I Corinthians 5:11; II John 11.
[44]II John 11.

⁴⁵II Thessalonians 3:6.
⁴⁶II Thessalonians 3:14.

Study Questions

1. Discuss the different levels of fellowship described in this chapter. Can you identify yourself in these?

2. Is it possible for brethren to strongly disagree and still be in fellowship?

3. Does fellowship always imply endorsement or approval? Discuss.

4. What does it mean to extend "the right hand of fellowship"?

5. Is there a proper procedure for practicing discipline?

6. What suggestions do you have for carrying out discipline?

7. If a brother refuses to repent when spoken to individually or with two or three witnesses, what good will it do to "tell it to the church?"

8. Who should lead in the practice of discipline in the local church?

13 / The Purposes of Discipline

"The neglect of discipline in the church is in reality a neglect of fellowship."

"It is a shallow and misguided love which prefers to let a brother go to hell rather than correct his wrong. Brotherly love cares enough to correct."

Fruits of Neglected Discipline

Discipline is not a policing process to make people conform to ecclesiastical rules. It is rather a caring correction, motivated by love. Instead of regarding discipline as disruptive to fellowship in the church, one must understand that only through discipline can true fellowship exist. The lack of discipline is one of the most effective tools of the devil. Because of its neglect, the church of Jesus Christ has experienced some crippling handicaps.

First, the neglect of discipline compromises the church's distinctiveness. If "anything goes," then "nothing matters." When one can believe anything he wants and act anyway he likes without affecting his fellowship in the church, there is no reason for the church to exist. It has lost its distinctiveness. It becomes no more than just another socio-political institution of man. Some church leaders who are moaning about the loss of distinctiveness in the church have themselves been major contributors to the process. They sowed the seeds of non-discipline and are now reaping the fruit of non-distinctiveness.

Second, the neglect of discipline has robbed the church of its evangelistic zeal. If one's faith is not important enough to die for, then it is not important enough to live for. If one will not affirm his faith in practice, then how can he be expected to affirm his faith in proclamation? The "proof of claim" of one's faith is its practice. If one does not believe in the teaching of Jesus strongly enough to support it through discipline in the church, how can he be expected to support it through evangelism outside the church?

Martin E. Marty has observed that some of the objections that have been made to missions are motivated by the loss of nerve:

> A "failure of nerve" in the Western Church has entered
> missionary discussion because it is felt that all
> attempts to extend the reconciling circle can be
> accomplished only at the expense of already valid forms
> of religion. Who gives Christians the right to assert
> the superiority of their religion?[1]

It is surprising that in all of the study of church growth which has taken place in the last two decades, so little has been said about church discipline. Church discipline is one of the basic principles of church growth. A church which practices loving discipline is a growing church because it has genuine conviction in its message. It has always been so. It was after the discipline of Ananias and Sapphira that Luke records:

> And great fear came upon the whole church, and upon
> all who heard of these things ...And all the more
> believers in the Lord, multitudes of men and women,
> were constantly added to their number.[2]

Church discipline will not destroy the church. It will rather strengthen its fellowship and increase its numbers.

Third, the neglect of discipline has caused many members of the church to surrender their commitment. How can one be committed to the teachings of Jesus if they are not important enough to affirm through corrective discipline in the church? A little leaven caused by undisciplined immorality and unrefuted error in the church will weaken the commitment of all of its members.

There will not be the restraining influence of the disapproval of the brethren. A faith which allows anything means nothing.

At a time in which there is a great concern in the church about declining numbers and dying congregations, one should not look for scapegoats of "worldly culture" and "old and ineffective methods" so much as the internal corruption resulting from the lack of discipline.

Reasons for Neglect

The neglect of church discipline is a real threat to meaningful fellowship in the church. Such neglect is to be found in churches that in many other ways are very zealous to teach the whole counsel of God. Why is it that there is such a great problem with this one aspect of Jesus' teaching? Four reasons are suggested.

First, the church neglects discipline because of fear. Some leaders are afraid of lawsuits.[3] Some are afraid of the response of the congregation if a popular brother is disciplined. Some are afraid to bring a problem out into the open, lest others become discouraged. In nearly all cases they are afraid of how others will respond to them and their leadership.

One cannot let "fear of men" keep him from his responsibility to God or the church. The voice of the people is not the voice of God. Those who are selected by the congregation as leaders should lead. Preachers, teachers or shepherds are not "up front" to parrot what the people want to hear or lead them where the multitude wants to go. Their responsibility is to lead them in the way of the Lord—no matter how unpopular or how painful this leadership will be.

John recorded with disfavor a situation within Jesus' ministry in which some men were afraid to act upon their convictions:

> Nevertheless many even of the rulers believed in Him,
> but because of the Pharisees they were not confessing
> Him, lest they should be put out of the synagogue; for
> they loved the approval of men rather than the
> approval of God.[4]

It is a shame when the fear of other men can influence a person more than the fear of God. Such betrays a lack of faith in God and His will.

Second, the church neglects discipline because of procrastination. When a wrongdoing needs immediate action, leaders in the church too often adopt an attitude of "wait and see." By the time they "wait and see" the effectiveness of discipline is gone.

Procrastination allows the sinner to go so far into sin that he is enslaved. His condition has worsened because nothing was done to recall him. Urgency is recommended by the Scriptures for those who become involved in sin:

> But encourage one another day after day, as long as it
> is still called "Today," lest any one of you be hardened
> by the deceitfulness of sin.[5]

Delay in correcting a brother in sin only allows the devil more time to enslave his will and harden his heart.

Procrastination allows the leaven of sin to spread to others in the congregation. What started as an isolated infection in only one member can cause the total body to be sick. Churches have been destroyed because error was not challenged when it was first known. Under the guise of "loving tolerance" the leaders refused to act and thus allowed the error to spread.

Foy Smith wrote of the importance of taking decisive action in church discipline in order to keep a sin from spreading:

> When a tree is pruned and kept in a healthy state it
> bears more fruit. When the rotten apple is thrown out
> of the peck the others are saved. When an infected
> member of the physical body is either restored or
> removed the entire body functions more perfectly.
> When the church is kept pure by pruning, weeding out,
> even by withdrawing in the extreme cases, it will grow
> as we have never seen it grow before.[6]

The road to hell is paved with good intentions which never were acted upon. To the painful sorrow of many leaders of the church, they have witnessed sin and error take over most or all of the congregation that they were supposed to be leading. They learned from experience that it is possible to do "too little — too late."

Third, the church neglects discipline because of a desire to conceal sin. They are ashamed of the sinner in the church and want to hide the evidence under the rug. Sin will not go away because one merely refuses to acknowledge it. It only becomes a stronger force and has a broader influence.

It is a delusion to think that sin is concealed merely because it is not dealt with openly. Generally it is already being whispered about in rumors. Rumors spoken in the shadows are often exaggerated or untrue. They are, however, able to do their evil work of causing confusion and disorder. The best way to dispel the darkness of a false rumor is to expose it to the light of truth. Truth seeks the light because it has nothing to conceal.

> But he who practices the truth comes to the light, that
> his deeds may be manifested as having been wrought
> in God.[7]

The need of confronting sin instead of concealing it is plainly shown in the case of Achan.[8] When Israel defeated Jericho, Achan kept some of the spoils of the city for himself. This was against the command of God who said:

> And the city shall be under the ban, it and all that is in
> it belongs to the Lord ...only keep yourselves from
> the things under the ban, lest you covet them and take
> some of the things under the ban, so would make
> the camp of Israel accursed and bring trouble on it.[9]

Because of the sin of Achan, Israel was defeated at Ai. Thirty-six men were killed. Joshua and all of Israel were discouraged. They had conquered the big city of Jericho with great ease, but they were defeated at the small town of Ai. Joshua complained to God because He had allowed them to be defeated. God answered and told him that the defeat was because there was "sin in the camp" of Israel.

> There are things under the ban in your midst, O Israel.
> You cannot stand before your enemies until you have
> removed the things under the ban from your midst.[10]

Joshua found that Achan had concealed gold, silver and a beautiful garment from the spoils of the city of Jericho. Joshua took Achan, his family and all his possessions and stoned them in the valley of Achor. When Israel removed the sin from their midst, God gave them victory.

As long as sin remained in the camp, there was defeat. God refused to help those who tolerated sin in their midst. Israel's toleration of Achan's sin made the whole nation guilty. By allowing sin in the camp, the whole nation became partakers in the sin.[11]

Because of Achan's sin many innocent people suffered. Thirty-six men died. His family was stoned with him. The whole army was defeated. All Israel was discouraged. When decisive action was taken and sin removed from Israel, then God blessed them with victory.

How many churches have found themselves in the same condition as Israel. They suffer defeat and wonder "Why?" They try to lay the blame on external factors, when they should be looking at "sin in the camp." Instead of showing unmerited toleration to the one guilty of sin, they should be concerned with the innocent who suffer because the sin is not removed.

It is folly for church leaders to think that by concealing sin, the church is better off. Members of the church can better deal with a brother who is living in sin through honest confrontation than by allowing the rumors of the uninformed to cause confusion.

Fourth, the church neglects discipline because leaders do not want to be placed in the position of being a judge. This is understandable. Jesus condemned judging:

> Do not judge lest you be judged yourselves. For in
> the way you judge, you will be judged; and by your
> standard of measure, it shall be measured to you.
> And why do you look at the speck in your brother's eye,
> but do not notice the log that is in your own eye? Or
> how can you say to your brother, "Let me take the speck
> out of your eye," and behold, the log is in your own eye?
> You hypocrite, first take the log out of your own eye;
> and then you will see clearly enough to take the speck
> out of your brother's eye.[12]

This passage does not condemn judging. It rather tells the consequence of judging. You will be judged like you judge. It tells how to judge. One must first rid himself of his own problems before he can do a good job of helping others get rid of their problems. In the same context, Jesus said two times, "you will know them by their fruits."[13] Jesus also qualifies the judging process by a statement recorded in John:

> Do not judge according to appearance, but judge with
> righteous judgment.[14]

The subjectivity can be taken out of judging. One only compares the objective conduct of a person's life with the objective standard of God revealed in the Scriptures. He is not placed in the position of a judge. He rather pronounces judgment that has already been made by God.

There are some sins that are difficult to detect. How can one know if one is guilty of pride? How can one prove that a brother is guilty of secret lust? How can one detect the sins of jealousy and hatred that are harbored in the heart? How can the sin of hypocrisy be discerned? God knows the presence of such sins in a person's life. The one who is guilty of such sins knows about them. Such sins do not become evident to others until they expose themselves through external actions. Only by their fruits can they be known.

Some sins are not evident to men. These sins might be secret sins of the heart. They have produced no external evidence in life or speech by which they can be exposed. God will judge such sins, but man cannot. Such sins cannot be disciplined by the church until they are exposed by speech or conduct.

Paul recognized that sins can only be exposed by the deeds that a man does. God knows the secrets of a man's heart. They will be revealed and punished at the judgment. Man, however, can only know about deeds that reveal sin in the heart:

> The sins of some men are quite evident, going before them
> to judgment; for others, their sins follow after. Likewise
> also, deeds that are good are quite evident, and those
> which are otherwise cannot be concealed.[15]

One cannot know the thoughts of a man's heart until they are revealed through his deeds. Jesus taught this principle:

> ...for the mouth speaks out of that which fills the heart.
> The good man out of his good treasure brings forth what
> is good; and the evil man out of his evil treasure brings
> forth what is evil.[16]

Sins of speech and conduct can be disciplined by the church. Immorality, blasphemy, swindling and stealing can be detected by men because they are sins of conduct. Sins of the heart are not so easily detected and judged. Men can be disciplined for them only when they are exposed by conduct.

Leaders are accountable to God for watching after the members of the church. They are the protectors of the fellowship. Like a shepherd who looks after his sheep, so should leaders of the church look after the flock of God. Elders are admonished to "shepherd the flock of God among you."[17] Members of the church are to submit to their leaders because they are responsible for watching over their souls:

> Obey your leaders, and submit to them; for they keep
> watch over your souls, as those who will give an account.
> Let them do this with joy and not with grief, for this
> would be unprofitable for you.[18]

Church leaders are not living up to their calling who neglect to watch out for all of the members of the church. This must be done even if it demands "caring enough to correct."

One of the qualifications of an overseer is the ability to recognize and refute error. This is clearly shown in Paul's instructions to Titus:

> ...holding fast the faithful word which is in
> accordance with the teaching, that he may be able both
> to exhort in sound doctrine and to refute those who
> contradict. For there are many rebellious men, empty
> talkers and deceivers, especially those of the circumcision,
> who must be silenced because they are upsetting whole
> families, teaching things they should not teach, for the
> sake of sordid gain.[19]

This passage shows several things about confronting error in the church. First, those who are overseers must be able to confront error. Such is one of their qualifications. It is a "cop out" of responsibility to suggest that leaders of the church have no role to play in refuting error or disciplining the immoral in the church.

Second, error is to be refuted on the basis of the word.[20] The word provides an objective criterion for determining error. No personal subjective opinion is involved. Only scriptures are involved. Leaders must know the word if they are to use it "to refute those who contradict." Ignorance of "sound doctrine" disqualifies one from being an overseer. Such is also true of a pseudo-tolerant spirit which refuses to confront false teachings.

Third, error tolerated will bring problems into the church. Whole families will be upset. Deceivers will lead astray those who are weak and untaught. Empty talkers will cause confusion. Tolerating error does not keep the peace;

it rather brings confusion into the church and will finally destroy it.

When sin is exposed in the church, it is not done by personal authority or private judgment. It is done by the authority of God as revealed in Scripture. No one has personal authority to discipline. If sin is exposed and the sinner disciplined, it is because the word of God has condemned the sin and the sinner has been rebellious. The process by which this is done is by Christians judging those who sin. Paul teaches this in the context of church discipline:

> For what have I to do with judging outsiders? Do you
> not judge those who are within the church? But those
> who are outside, God judges...[21]

It is just as wrong to neglect the responsibility of judging righteous judgment as it is to presumptuously and hypocritically judge according to appearance.

Three Purposes

The Scriptures are clear about the purposes of discipline in the church. Paul stated them when he instructed the church at Corinth to discipline an immoral brother:

> In the name of our Lord Jesus, when you are assembled,
> and I with you in spirit, with the power of our Lord
> Jesus, I decided to deliver such a one to Satan for the
> destruction of his flesh, that his spirit may be
> saved in the day of the Lord Jesus. Your boasting is not
> good. Do you not know that a little leaven leavens
> the whole lump of dough? Clean out the old leaven,
> that you may be a new lump, just as you are in fact
> unleavened. For Christ our Passover also has been
> sacrificed.[22]

The context of this passage is that there was an immoral brother in the church at Corinth who was not being disciplined for his conduct. In fact, the church was "puffed up" in pride about their tolerant attitude. Paul rebuked them and instructed them about what to do and why they were to do it.

They were to deliver the immoral brother to Satan. It was to be done in the name of the the Lord Jesus. The purposes were threefold. The bold type of the text above reveals them. First, it was to recall the immoral brother from his sin and save his soul. Second, it was to keep the sin from spreading to others in the church. Third, it was to preserve the holiness of the church.

The first purpose of church discipline is to save the sinner. If he is not confronted and his sin is not exposed, he will not change. He will remain in sin and be lost. Christian brothers cannot stand by and allow this to happen. The purpose of discipline is basically for the good of the sinner.

Discipline might be painful to his ego and hurtful to his pride right now, but it is necessary if he is to be recalled from his sin. Only such drastic action can break his heart and lead him to repentance. It is difficult for such a brother to be cut off from the fellowship of the church. One must, however, be more concerned about his eternal salvation than he is for his personal feelings. It is a shallow and misguided love which prefers to let a brother go to hell rather than correct his wrong. Brotherly love cares enough to correct.

How many have been lost because there was not sufficient fellowship in the church to discipline a brother in sin? The consequence of neglecting discipline is lost souls. James shows the necessity of such confrontive discipline in the church:

> My brethren, if any among you strays from the truth,
> and one turns him back; let him know that he who
> turns a sinner from the error of his way will save
> his soul from death, and will cover a multitude of
> sins.[23]

Not only does the Scripture reveal how and why discipline is to be administered in the church. It also gives a case history to show that it works. One cannot be sure that II Corinthians is talking about the same brother who was disciplined in I Corinthians 5, but it is likely so. At least, some brother who was known by both Paul and the Corinthians had been disciplined by the church. The discipline had caused him to be convicted of sin and repent. There was some kind of problem in the church about receiving him back into the fellowship. Paul gave instructions on what they were to do:

> Sufficient for such a one is this punishment which
> was inflicted by the majority, so that on the contrary
> you should rather forgive and comfort him, lest
> somehow such a one be overwhelmed by excessive
> sorrow.[24]

188

Corrective discipline worked at Corinth in the first century; it will also work today in recalling Christians who are involved in sin. It was the "punishment inflicted by the majority" that forced the issue with the erring brother. He had to choose between God or the devil — righteousness or sin. The discipline forced him to make a choice.

The second purpose of discipline is to keep the sin from spreading. A proverb is quoted: "A little leaven leavens the whole lump of dough." If leaven is placed in a lump of dough, it will soon leaven the whole. The only way to stop the leavening process is to take the leaven out of the dough. Paul applies this proverb to the situation at Corinth. If sin is tolerated in one member of the church, it will soon spread to all of the church. First, only one was guilty of the sin, but soon the whole church will be. Refusal of fellowship is necessary so as not to share in the sins of others.[25]

Such has been the experience of numerous congregations. In the name of "liberty," sin is tolerated. Under the guise of "love," sin is ignored. With the pretense of "humility," sin is not corrected. The result is that sin spreads. What started out as the sinful practice of one now becomes the sinful practice of others. The sin spreads and the permissive spirit which allowed the sin to go undisciplined also spreads. No sin can consistently be confronted without dealing with a whole backlog of sins formerly tolerated by the church. The result is "nothing is done." Souls are lost and the sin keeps spreading.

Paul warns of the same kind of leavening influence from false teachers:

> ...and their talk will spread like gangrene,
> among whom are Hymenaeus and Philetus, men
> who have gone astray from the truth saying that
> the resurrection has already taken place, and thus
> upset the faith of some.[26]

False teachers are compared to gangrene in the above passage. They should be treated as gangrene. If a person has gangrene in one of his feet he does not need a pain killer, he needs radical surgery. If a congregation has a false teacher in the fellowship, it does not need to glory in the openness of its fellowship, it needs to exercise discipline.

The author knows of a number of churches who have become sectarian because false teachers were tolerated and undisciplined. False teachers, even though their personality might seem very personable and kind, cause division. If they believe a false doctrine, they have to teach it. If they teach it, it will cause a party to form. Division is the result. Paul warned the elders at Ephesus about such false teachers:

Be on guard for yourselves and for all the flock, among
which the Holy Spirit has made you overseers, to
shepherd the church of God which He purchased with
His own blood. I know that after my departure savage
wolves will come in among you, not sparing the flock;
and from among your own selves men will arise,
speaking perverse things, to draw away the disciples
after them. Therefore be on the alert.[27]

False teachers are not to receive sympathy because leaders of the church
opposed them. They are dangerous like wolves in a flock of sheep. A wolf does
not visit a sheep pasture because he likes the company of sheep. He has more
destructive ideas on his mind.

For the good of the church, discipline must be practiced. There is no other
way to keep sin and error from becoming a cancer to consume its life's blood.

A third purpose of discipline is to maintain the holiness of the church.
Withdrawal of fellowship is necessary to preserve church identity. Everett
Ferguson has identifed this purpose:

When the reflection of Christ by the church is damaged
by someone, the church must withdraw from him.[28]

Paul's statement to the Corinthians to "clean out the old leaven" is an analogy
from the Jewish practice of taking leaven out of the house at the feast of
unleavened bread. Every bit of leaven was to be cleaned out "that you may be
a new lump." The analogy identifies the "lump" as being the church. Paul is
teaching that "the leavening influence of sin" must be taken out of the church
that it may be holy and uncontaminated.

The church is holy. It is the temple of the Holy Spirit and like the temple
of God at Jerusalem, it is holy.[29] It was purchased by the blood of Jesus Christ
and is the holy bride of Christ.[30] Sin contaminates the holiness of the church and
must not be tolerated.

Sin desecrates the temple of God. Just as Jesus expelled those who
desecrated the holy temple at Jerusalem,[31] so should His disciples defend the
sanctity of the church.

Sin defiles the bride of Christ. Jesus desires His bride to be "holy and
without blemish." When undisciplined sin is tolerated in the church, "the way
of truth will be maligned."[32] The purity and holiness of the church should be
the desire of every Christian:

I love thy kingdom, Lord, The house of Thine abode;
The church our blest Redeemer saved with His own precious blood,
I love Thy church, O God! Her walls before Thee stand,
Dear as the apple of Thine eye, and graven on thy hand.[33]

The threefold purpose of discipline in the church is to save the sinner from hell, to keep sin from spreading to others and to maintain the holiness of the church.

When Discipline Fails

What about those times when it seems that church discipline fails to accomplish its purposes? The sinner has not come to repentance, the leavening influence of sin has not yet been removed from the church and it would appear that the church has lost its holiness. The noble purposes of discipline have not been accomplished.

Maybe no, but maybe so! What appears to be failure may be only a temporary setback. It would be difficult to convince one who believed in doing things according to the Scriptures that God's way ever fails.

It is true that God's way does not always produce the kind of response He wants from man. After all, God is "not wishing for any to perish but for all to come to repentance,"[34] yet men still go against the will of God and will be lost. The fact that the plan of God — in bringing salvation — did not bring repentance in all men does not invalidate it. It only shows that man is free to choose.

If it appears that discipline failed to bring the brother to repentance, look for the other purposes. Did discipline keep the sin from spreading to others? Did discipline maintain the integrity of the church in opposing sin? Did discipline instill fear into others and keep them from sinning?

If it appears that discipline failed, look for some of the possible causes. Was it because fellowship was not strong enough to persuade the sinning brother? Was it because the right pattern of conduct or the right attitude of administration was not followed? Was it because the sinner's heart was just too hard or his sin too enslaving and it was impossible to renew him again to repentance?

If it appears that discipline has failed, be patient. Maybe the process is not yet finished. It took some time for the devil to enslave the erring brother and it might take some time for the chains to be broken. Maybe God is not through working with this brother. He might become another Saul of Tarsus once he is convicted of his sins.

Restoring Discipline to Fellowship

The neglect of discipline in the church is in reality a neglect of fellowship. Discipline is only effective when fellowship is strong. Fellowship is strong only when discipline is practiced. One cannot have one without the other.

Discipline is the strongest expression of fellowship in Christ. It can only exist when one cares enough for his brother to correct his wrongdoing. Genuine fellowship in Christ cannot exist without discipline any more than love can exist without expression.

There is much to do in restoring the kind of fellowship which existed in the early church. Human barriers must be torn down. Permissiveness which ignores the limits of fellowship must be exposed. God's family must repent of their indifference to the brotherhood needs and their lack of brotherly love. Fellowship restoration must also include the responsibility of discipline.

Perhaps no words can better speak of the need of restoring fellowship to the church, than those given by Paul:

> Now if you have known anything of Christ's encouragement
> and of his reassuring love; if you have known something
> of the fellowship of his Spirit, and of compassion
> and deep sympathy, do make my joy complete —
> live together in harmony, live together
> in love, as though you had only one mind and one spirit
> between you. Never act from motives of rivalry or
> personal vanity, but in humility think more of each other
> than you do of yourselves. None of you should think only
> of his own affairs, but consider other people's interests also.
> Let your attitude to life be that of Christ Jesus himself.[35]

Fellowship in the church finds its theological basis in the Divine relationship that each child of God has with his Heavenly Father. This fellowship finds expression in the faith, the practices and even the attitudes demonstrated in "our life together" in the church. Fellowship in the church is a place of tough and tender love. The relationship is tender enough for each brother to regard the other as more important than himself. The relationship is tough enough that those who are overcome by sin and deceived by error are disciplined. Those who are brothers and sisters in the family of God care enough to correct.

Endnotes

[1]Marty E. Martin, *Church Unity and Church Mission* (Grand Rapids: Wm B. Eerdmans Publishing Co., 1964), p.136.

[2]Acts 5:11, 14.

[3]See page 146, footnote #2.

[4]John 12:42-43.

[5]Hebrews 3:13.

[6]Ed Smithson, *The Forgotten Commandment* (Moore, Oklahoma: Ed Smithson, 1965), Foreword by Foy Smith.

[7]John 3:21.

[8]Joshua 7:1-26.

[9]Joshua 6:17-18.

[10]Joshua 7:13.

[11]See II John 10-11.

[12]Matthew 7:1-5.

[13]Matthew 7:16, 20.

[14]John 7:24.

[15]I Timothy 5:24-25.

[16]Matthew 12:34-35.

[17]I Peter 5:1-2.

[18]Hebrews 13:17.

[19]Titus 1:9-11.

[20]It should be noted that "faithful word", "teaching" and "sound doctrine" are equated in the text.

[21]I Corinthians 5:12-13.

[22]I Corinthians 5:4-7. The bold face type is by the author to emphasize the purposes of discipline contained in the text.

[23]James 5:19-20.

[24]II Corinthians 2:6-8.

[25]I Timothy 5:22; Ephesians 5:11.

[26]II Timothy 2:17-18.

[27]Acts 20:28-31.

[28]Everett Ferguson, *The New Testament Church* (Abilene: Biblical Research Press, 1968), p. 44.

[29]I Corinthians 3:16-17.

[30]Ephesians 5:27.

[31]Matthew 21:12-13.

[32]II Peter 2:2.

[33]From the song, "I Love Thy Kingdom, Lord" by Timothy Dwight.
[34]II Peter 3:9.
[35]Philippians 2:1-5 in Phillips Paraphrase.

Study Questions

1. Discuss the "fruits of neglected discipline."

2. What is the purpose of discipline?

3. What if discipline fails, then what do you do?

4. "We are not to judge" is often used as a reason why we should not practice discipline. How would you respond?

5. How has the neglect of discipline affected the church's distinctiveness?

6. In what ways has the lack of discipline caused our failure in evangelistic power?

7. Why do you suppose there is a failure to practice discipline in the local church?

8. "We can never become everything God wants us to be until we restore the practice of discipline in the local church." Would you agree or disagree? Discuss.

Printed in the United States
6826

9 780892 254699